Cool Mac®
Animation
Second Edition

Sean Wagstaff

Hayden
Books

Cool Mac Animation, Second Edition

© 1994 Hayden Books, a division of Prentice Hall Computer Publishing.

Library of Congress Catalog Number: 93-80003

ISBN: 0-672-068-9

96 95 94   4 3 2 1

Interpretation of the printing code: the rightmost double-digit number is the year of the book's printing; the rightmost single-digit number is the number of the book's printing. For example, a printing code of 94-1 shows that the first printing of the book occurred in 1994.

For my cool brother,
Mike Wagstaff

Publisher	David Rogelberg
Acquisition Editor	Karen Whitehouse
Development Editor	Brad Miser
Technical Reviewer	Ben Long
Copy/Production Editor	Marj Hopper
Cover Designer	Jay Corpus
Interior Designer	Barbara Webster
Production Analyst	Mary Beth Wakefield
Production Team	Gary Adair
	Angela Bannan
	Katy Bodenmiller
	Brad Chinn
	Jeanne Clark
	Kim Cofer
	Meshell Dinn
	Mark Enochs
	Stephanie Gregory
	Jenny Kucera
	Beth Rago
	Marc Shecter
	Kris Simmons
	Greg Simsic
	Carol Stamile
	Robert Wolf

Composed in ITC Garamond, Helvetica, and MCPdigital by Hayden.

About the Author

Sean Wagstaff is a former editor of *Wind Surf* and *California Angler* magazines, and he recently left his three-year post as associate reviews editor of *MacWEEK* to pursue a career as a free-lancer. His first book, *Macintosh 3-D Workshop*, hit the shelves late in 1993. He now creates wickedly cool video animations and 3-D and 2-D illustrations, authors multimedia CD-ROMs, writes hard-hitting reviews of multimedia software, and snowboards, windsurfs, and otherwise loves life as time allows. When he's not hunched over his "chrome-package-power-everything-4WD" Quadra 950, Sean can sometimes be found working with a PowerBook and Wacom tablet in his '75 camper.

Contact him via CompuServe at:

72102, 2466

Overview

Contents

viii

Acknowledgements

My sincere appreciation to the team at Hayden Books for keeping it coming at me. Without RoseAnn and Boris at the VALIS Group, this project wouldn't have gotten off the ground; their software is still the coolest thing going. Thanks to Ethan Watters, Joe Conlin, and my father, Thomas Wagstaff, the people who got me started in this writing gig in the first place. Thanks to many of my eternally hip friends: Jim Humes and Big Jim, Jeff, Pete, Anne, Neil, Sonja, Po, Nina, Sam, Kirsten (and Dylan), Ben, Cynthia, Dorit—and anyone else who's contributed a cheerful mug to the cause. Thanks Mom, for being so strong.

Sean Wagstaff
February, 1994

To Our Readers

Dear Friend,

I want to thank you on behalf of everyone at Hayden Books for choosing *Cool Mac Animation, Second Edition* to help you learn the basics of using the Mac to create your own animations. We know that it can be difficult to learn something new without the right assistance. We have carefully crafted this book to make it effective in helping you learn to animate on the Mac, while allowing you to have *fun* at the same time.

What our readers think of our books is important to our ability to better serve you in the future. If you have any comments, no matter how great or small, we'd appreciate you taking the time to send us a note. Of course, great book ideas are always welcome.

Sincerely yours,

David Rogelberg
Publisher, Hayden Books and Adobe Press

You can reach Hayden Books at the following:

Hayden Books
201 West 103rd Street
Indianapolis, IN 46290
(800) 428-5331 voice
(800) 448-3804 fax

E-mail addresses:

America Online: HaydenBks
AppleLink: hayden.books
CompuServe: 76350,3014
Internet: hayden@hayden.com

Conventions Used in This Book

Text you are required to type appears in a `special typeface`.

Menu names and menu options appear in the bold version of the same **`special typeface`**.

The names of specific files and folders appear in "quotation marks."

Keystroke combinations are indicated as in the following example:

Press Command-P to print.

This means you press and hold the Command key (the key at the bottom of your keyboard with pictures of an apple and a cloverleaf on it) and then press the P key. Release both keys simultaneously.

Cool Mac

1

Introduction

Check this out—The Stealth Submarine meets Moby Dick: of thermonuclear subsonic proportions. Wouldn't it be awesome if you could make it on your Mac?

You can, and it will be cool. Totally.

But I know you're thinking, "I'm destitutionally, utterly, pennilessly, completely bankrupt. You know what I mean? Too broke for a Coke. Can I still do worthy Mac animation?"

Absolutely. Everything you need, except for the Mac, comes with this book. That includes a demo version of a completely cool animation and special effects program called Flo' and Apple's QuickTime extension (free!). Of course, *Cool Mac Animation* also explains what's out there in terms of really cool (but cheap) commercial animation software for starving artists like yourself.

But you say you only have a C- in brainiology? Are you hopeless *and* clueless?

Nope. It's OK if you're developmentally undistinguished. In fact, mondo animations are cake as long as you're sufficiently smart to read this book. *Cool Mac Animation* teaches you everything you need to know to do killer cartoons.

What if your Mac is, you know, practically an antique—you've had it since last year. It doesn't even have a holoconferencing synthesizer on the motherboard.

Have a chill pill, Bill. *Cool Mac Animation* is backwardly-compatible with vacuum tubes, Precambrian stone axes, early Macintosh computers, and other prehistoric number crunchers. Of course, animation gets even more heliofrigorific when you have Multiprocessing-NoDuh networks at your disposal. But that doesn't mean nanoneurological GFLOP CPUs are mandatory to crank out psycho stuff. You can do cool Mac animation with just about any Mac capable of running QuickTime (SE/30 or later). In some cases, you can even do animation without one of the newer Macs.

What do you need to get started?

You're looking at it: *Cool Mac Animation, Second Edition*.

What Is Cool Mac Animation?

This book is a first step for anyone interested in delving into the strange and wonderful world of computer animation. It begins with the basic principles of creating animation itself: cels, frames, onion-skinning, registration, layering, and many of the basic aesthetics of animation. Then it covers the sometimes complicated world of what you need to know to successfully create animations on the Mac. File formats such as QuickTime, PICS, and PACo are explained; digitizing video, drawing tablets, playback performance, disk space, memory constraints, and other hardware issues are also covered.

Most importantly, *Cool Mac Animation* serves as a guide to many low-cost, cool commercial and shareware software programs (averaging under $200) for creating the *coolest* Mac animations.

Having to pay megatons of money for software isn't cool, so *Cool Mac Animation* concentrates on software that costs 300 bucks or less. In special cases, we've made exceptions to talk about programs that cost as much as $500. Keep in mind though, professional animators sometimes use software that's in the $1,000 price range or even higher. If you've got that kind of money to spend on software, you're probably too badly hooked on animation for the less ambitious likes of this book.

2

What's on the Cool Animation Disk

The *Cool Animation Disk*, the free high-density disk that comes with this book, includes a demo version of the VALIS Group's Flo', a really unique and creative animation program. This demo version of Flo' was created especially for *Cool Mac Animation*! Even better, we've included a good-size collection of wacky and original digitized photographs to use with the program.

Flo'

Flo' is one of the weirdest and most original Mac animation programs in existence and we're psyched to be able to include a working demo version of the program on the *Cool Animation Disk*. On the surface, Flo' is really simple. Imagine you have a photograph printed on an infinitely flexible rubber sheet that you can warp, stretch, and twist in any way you choose. Flo' lets you do this. You can also set *key frames* for each new distortion and Flo' will automatically create an animation where the image flows smoothly from one distorted state to the next. The effect is sort of like having a molten photograph; it's hilarious and utterly cool. We think of Flo' as a fun house for the Mac.

Incidentally, much of the flip book animation in the upper-right corner of the right-hand pages of this book was created using Flo'—just to get you inspired.

In addition, there's a folder full of digital photographs, including some from *Wayne's World* and *The Addams Family*, you can use for creating your own animations with Flo'.

QuickTime

To ensure that you can have plenty of fun with the movies you create, we've also included the latest version of the QuickTime extension and Apple's Movie Player.

Flo' saves its animations as QuickTime movies which you can play with the Movie Player, or you can easily incorporate your Flo' animations into other multimedia projects.

A Brief History of Yosemite Sam and Company

Since the beginning of time (your Mac will tell you time began on Jan. 1, 1904, but it was actually even earlier), people have communicated by using sequences of pictures. Ancient Egyptians (according to my mummy) and Stone Age man (no, *not* the Rolling Stones, although they have been around a long time, too) all started out by scratching pictures on the wall. City dwellers usually recognize this art form as graffiti, not realizing that it's really an ancient form of animation.

Animation really got the dust blown off it in the 1800s when a series of theories and experiments helped to prove the principle of "persistence of vision." Essentially, so the theory goes, the eye sees in snapshots taken a small fraction of a second apart. Each of these images persists on the retina until the next snapshot. One test of this effect is to flash a bright light in your face while standing in a dark room. You'll notice a bright "hot spot" that slowly fades away in the dark, even though the actual light source is present for only a moment.

The scientists who set out to prove this theory first invented the *stroboscope* and then the *zeotrope*. These were primitive toys, when compared to big-screen TVs, that allowed people to view a series of sequential drawings through slots in a spinning disk or through a simple shutter. Nevertheless, they became popular doodads in their day because people were so enamored with the idea of animated pictures.

Early animation machines relied on hand drawings. The use of photographic animations (what came to be called "movies") wasn't practical, because photographs were made on fragile metal or glass plates and required lengthy exposures. (Have you ever wondered why nineteenth century photos always feature tight-lipped, bummed out looking people? It's probably because they had to sit holding their breath for so long.)

In the 1870s a guy named Jules Marey invented a camera that looked exactly like a big shotgun. It took pictures in a row on a circular disk, enabling him to capture the motion of birds' wings, among other things (apparently, he liked to shoot birds).

About the same time, a series of photographs by Eadweard Muybridge were the first thing that really resembled modern movies. He set up long rows of cameras (with whopping 1/1000-second shutter speeds) triggered by trip wires along the side of a racetrack and then had horses gallop past. The series of pictures he took was intended to settle a $25,000 bet made by Leland Stanford (as in the university) as to whether all of a horse's hooves leave the ground when it gallops. (Thanks to Ed, we know that they do.) Muybridge was intrigued by the results of his invention and soon turned it on people running by in pajamas, and other unusual motion studies. His photographs were the first of their kind and they caused a popular sensation.

The invention of high-speed celluloid film changed everything. (For instance, we now know how many times a hummingbird's wings beat in a second.)

Thomas A. Edison invented a camera called a *kinetograph* that would capture sequences of pictures on a long strip of film in individual *frames*. Because of the higher film speeds, it was possible to photograph as many as ten frames per second, enough to create the appearance of continuous smooth motion; and because the celluloid was transparent, it could be projected with Edison's companion invention, the *kinetoscope*—the first movie projector. (Light bulbs and sound recording, too—good ol' Alva was a multimedia dude way before his time!) Of course, movies became an instant success and it wasn't long before movie-making was refined from a science to an art.

While he wasn't the first animator, in the 1920s an artist named Walt Disney turned the clock back to popular science. Taking a cue from prehistoric cave dwellers, Disney started painting sequential pictures. The difference, however, was that Disney then transferred each of his painted pictures onto the frames of movie film. It didn't matter that the subjects he painted were animals which had never been hunted, idolized, or domesticated (the traditional subjects for cave paintings and hieroglyphs), Disney's menagerie was a phenomenon of Mickey Mouse proportions.

The rest, of course, is history, at least according to Bugs Bunny, Fred Flintstone, Bart Simpson, and Beavis & Butthead. Animation became the coolest new art form for fantasy and storytelling.

An entirely new way of animating has been evolving since the late 1970s. Instead of painting on plastic cels and filming the result, animators are busy creating their work on the flickering screens of computers. Computers merge traditional animation using hand-painted cels and live filmmaking that relies on photographic techniques. No longer are animators limited to 2-D drawings; instead they can paint on photographic images or merge photographic images with painted frames. Using the processing power of computers, photographic images can twisted, stretched, warped, and even metamorphosized in ways that defy description as either film *or* animation. For our part, we'll call any moving pictures animation; we'll deal with different styles as they come up.

A company called Industrial Light and Magic (ILM, creative studio of *Star Wars* director George Lucas) has defined a whole new bizarre and horrifyingly wonderful kind of animation—3-D. Realistic models of liquid robots, fantastic spaceships, alien worlds, even terrible dinosaurs, are now alive and traipsing through our psyches on a daily basis. ILM's most ambitious computer-animated movie was *Jurassic Park*—the most successful movie of all time.

Software makers have caught on to all this supernatural stomping about and have responded by creating low-cost software that brings traditional animation and cool new animation techniques into the realm of the average computer hacker.

All of which brings us to the here and now, and your Cool Mac. The eventual fallout from a century-and-a-half of animated hyperactivity is that personal computers—Macintoshes in particular—are now powerful enough, when equipped with the right software and a little know-how, to create animations of mega-cool proportions.

How Animation Works

As we said earlier, animation relies on persistence of vision to carry one frame of a movie smoothly into the next, with the result being that everything appears to flow along without interruption.

But how are animations created?

Usually, animators begin with a *script*. This is essentially a story that includes descriptions of action, dialog, and even cues for sound effects. Like any movie, a good animation begins with a good script.

Usually the script is adapted into a *storyboard*—a series of sketches that define the action in the animation. A storyboard looks a lot like a comic strip. This is used to stage different scenes, showing important changes in the scenery and showing which characters are present from scene-to-scene. It also provides a clearer idea of the movie's action.

One of the most important parts of creating a cartoon comes next: making the sound track. If your movie will have dialog, you'll need actors to act it out. (The late Mel Blanc was the most famous of all cartoon actors; his was the voice of Bugs Bunny, Daffy Duck, and many other instantly "wecognizable cowactas.") This may also be the point where you add sound effects such as background noises, explosions, music, and so on. (We include some tips for recording sounds for QuickTime productions later in this book.)

Once you've recorded a sound track, the next step is to create your characters in detail. Essentially, this is a series of drawings that show your character in many different poses and expressions. Professional animators call these detail drawings *model sheets* . Whenever you want to know how your character will look in a certain situation, you can refer to the model sheets. This is crucial if you have multiple artists working on a single animation, because they can all work on different parts of the movie while maintaining consistent characters.

When working in a traditional animation studio, animators go through a few more steps that really aren't part of the computer animation process: these include filming the storyboard in synch with the soundtrack, developing line tests (drawings that define all the action of the animation), painting cels (these are line drawings on clear acetate which can be filmed over backgrounds), and painting the backgrounds themselves. Finally, the cels are filmed against the backgrounds one frame at a time and synched with the soundtrack.

An important consideration in the creation of cels is *registration*. Simply put, this is the point on each cel that precisely aligns to a corresponding point on every other cel. This is required to keep each cel in proper relationship to the ones that come before and after it. One reason to use registration is to maintain relationships between moving objects. Remember Michael Jackson's Moon Walk? The reason this was so weird looking is that while he appeared to be walking normally, he'd actually slide backwards along the floor. While this effect may be desirable when break dancing and other unusual circumstances, you usually want your characters to move forward when they walk, flap their wings, roll, bound, or whatever. Registration plays a vital role in maintaining this appearance.

When animating to film, the standard *frame rate* is 24 frames per second. That means a 60-second animation has 1,440 individual frames. When working with video, the number of required frames is even higher—30 frames per second or 1,800 frames per minute. Keep in mind that most animations use separate cels for every character and that you'll often have several characters in a single scene. Three characters in a one minute video would require 5,400 cels. That's a lot of cels—and it's also probably the best reason to use computers to speed up the animation process. Another special reason for using computers instead of older methods is *layering*. For every cel using traditional techniques, you have to add another layer of acetate over the background. Most animators limit the number of layers to 5 or so, because acetate isn't perfectly clear; it begins to fog over the background and bottom layers as you add more of them. Computer animation, in contrast, doesn't have this problem. You can use an infinite number of layers without diminishing quality.

Mac Versus Old-Style Animation

Many of the techniques of traditional animation are directly adaptable to animation you'll do on the Mac. On the other hand, a lot of the tedious work is taken care of for you.

For example, cel-based animation programs allow you to use a technique called *onion-skinning*. (The name comes from the many layers in an onion's skin) or *ghosting*. While you're working on one cel of the animation you can view a dimmed version of the previous or next cel through your drawing surface. This lets you trace over the previous cel, changing only the parts that you want to change. The advantage of using a computer for this is that you can simply copy the contents of one cel and paste them into another, then modify the copy. This can save you oodles of drawing and painting time.

Cel animation programs also take care of all of the details for you, such as keeping all your cels in order, saving each character, and allowing you to instantly play back and step through parts of your production.

Layering is also handled automatically. You can move characters and background props up and down in the hierarchy, and you can move characters and backgrounds using *path animation*. Unlike cel animation, which relies on changes between painted frames, path animation allows you to define starting and ending points for a character and the program automatically *tweens* the character's position (meaning it calculates all of the positions between the two end points). Tweening can also be used for effects like stretching, squashing, and rotating. In the case of realistic 3-D software, tweening can even be used to smoothly blend one shape into another or one surface into the next.

Another feature related to path animation is *cycling*. A cel-based animation can be set to cycle, or *loop*, cels showing a specific activity over and over. For example, cels showing a character skipping can be looped so that when her travel plans need to change from a short trip next door to a longer journey through the woods, her animators don't have to spend a lot of time making it possible.

Of course, the Mac offers many other advantages, among them: digital painting tools; powerful editing software for combining animations with sound tracks; the capability to Undo anything you wish you hadn't done; and freedom from the huge expense of cameras, film, and the other costly tools of the traditional animator's trade.

And what's more, the Mac is easy to use and lots of fun.

Indefinable Animation

Mac animators not only have tools that make the task of animation much easier, but they also have at their fingertips programs that can do things the Warner brothers never dreamed of. Through digital processing of images—either ones you draw on the computer or scan in—it's possible to create animations that completely defy traditional animation techniques. These include things like morphing, warping, and 3-D. These processes rely on the liquefaction of image pixels or the intensive calculation of perspective and light, rather than frame-by-frame cel animation.

You can digitize video using a QuickTime capture board, then use the resulting frames of digital video as a starting point for a whole world of special effects. Some programs even allow you to paint over individual frames of video, a process known as *rotoscoping* .

Getting It All Out

It's one thing to create animation on a Mac, it's another to get it onto film and before the faces of an audience. A traditional animator shoots painted cels directly onto film, but it's another matter to get Mac-generated animations onto film or video. You can't simply film the Mac screen—there's far too much loss of image quality. Professional computer animators, therefore, rely on a technique called *device control* . The required software and special hardware steps an expensive *animation deck* one frame-at-a-time through an animation as it records the frames onto video. Fortunately, many service bureaus can do this for you. Simply bring them your finished animation as a standard Mac file.

On the other hand, the Mac itself can be used as a delivery mechanism—think of it as a really expensive, elaborate television with a small screen. You can play back Mac animations directly by themselves, or within the context of all kinds of cool multimedia productions.

Summary

Animation has come a long way from painting individual cels and photographing them with a camera, although for many animators these techniques are still common. Computer animators combine all kinds of images, using the Mac as a kind of instant-access movie camera, and they take advantage of the Mac's capability of pushing pixels around like putty.

The following chapter, "Animation Hardware," explains what you'll need to enter this world of fluid pictures.

CHAPTER

Cool Mac

Animation Hardware

By late 1993, Mac hardware had tumbled in price and increased in relative power, meaning a Mac you buy today is many times more powerful than a Mac you bought for the same amount a year or two ago. New machines like the Quadras have tools like built-in audio capture, and the "AV" Macs even have QuickTime video capture capabilities. However, the most important feature of the newer, faster Macs is that they're much better able to cope with the processing demands of computer animation. Techniques like morphing and 3-D rendering require a lot of number crunching, and when you're doing it dozens, hundreds, or even thousands of frames at a time, a fast computer helps. Since no book can adequately keep up with the ever-changing model numbers, we'll refrain from saying which Macs are OK for animation and which aren't; there are simply too many models with too many variables. However, the most important of those variables are explained here, so at least you'll know what you're dealing with.

11

Mac Models

In general, these are things to look for if your shopping around for a Mac to use for animation:

- **Processor.** The faster the Mac, the happier you'll be using it. But how fast is fast? The simplest measure of a Mac's speed is its processor. The oldest Macs used the Motorola 68000 chip as the main processor (sometimes called the CPU). This was followed by the 68020, the 68030, and the 68040, in that order. The newer processors, particularly the '040, are significantly faster than the older ones. A Mac Classic is an example of an old, slow 68000; a Quadra 840 AV is an excellent example of a fast 68040.

- **Clock speed.** Another measure of the Mac's raw computing power is the *clock speed*. This refers to the crystal, like something from the Starship Enterprise, that controls the number of times in a second the processor completes a cycle of calculations. The oldest Macs were clocked at 8 MHz (8,000 cycles per second). Newer Macs top out at 40 or even 50 MHz. Similar CPUs have performance directly proportional to their clock speed, so a 25 MHz processor is half as fast as a 50 MHz model. (A Quadra 840 AV is a 40 MHz '040).

- **FPU.** Another factor that affects a Mac's speed is the presence of a Floating Point Unit (FPU), commonly known as a math coprocessor. While an FPU doesn't impact the speed of the Mac for normal system functions, it has a dramatic effect on math calculations, and for the purposes of the Mac animator, this is extremely important because many special effects and features including rotation, resizing, and filtering of images rely directly on floating-point math functions. Some graphics software is so dependent on an FPU that it won't run without one.

- **Age.** All things being equal, newer Macs are faster than older ones. Apple is constantly updating things like memory caching and interleaving, SCSI access, and bus bottlenecks to milk that last drop of speed out of them.

System Memory

Random-access memory (*RAM*) is one of the most precious commodities you can load into your Mac. Current Mac models come with a minimum of 4M of RAM (a *megabyte* is one million *bytes*, or 8 million bits). Serious animators have their Mac loaded with at least 8M, often more. System 7 alone requires about 2M of RAM. Animation software will sometimes just barely run in a 2M partition, but if you're going to do anything particularly complicated, it will often require 4M or more. Complex 3-D software and QuickTime editors often require 6 or 8M. Keep in mind if the System requires 2M of RAM and your

software needs 6, you'll need 8M total. Since RAM is the part of your Mac that most resembles brains, it's definitely worth loading up as much as you can possibly afford.

Tip:
If you don't have enough RAM to run your software, you can use System 7's Virtual Memory to increase the apparent amount of RAM available to your Mac. Since this is using the hard disk to imitate memory, however, it's much, much slower than using real RAM. It also uses up disk space.

Hard Disk

Every Mac needs a hard disk, and the rule of thumb is the bigger the better. If you're willing to spend quite a bit of time backing things up to floppies or some other storage medium, a 40M hard disk is probably adequate. 80M or more of disk storage is nearly mandatory if you plan to do any serious video digitizing or other complex graphics, such as QuickTime animation, using a program like Flo'.

All but the very oldest Macs allow you to upgrade your Mac with an external SCSI drive. This is a disk drive that plugs into your Mac via a special cable, and it's an excellent way to upgrade a Mac, because you can always move the drive to another machine if you upgrade.

Tip:
If you're adding a new external hard disk to your system, pay special attention to the manufacturer's directions about SCSI ID and termination. If you don't get these right, your Mac will seem to have lost its mind.

The current standard hard drives are fast enough for most animation purposes. However, digitizing and playback of full-screen, full-motion video requires extra-fast array drives. These are actually two or more disks that pretend to be a single drive.

Color Hardware

The days of the black-and-white Mac are gone. Every new Macintosh, even PowerBooks, comes with some kind of color monitor support. The real distinction now is between 8-bit color systems and photorealistic 24-bit color. While desktop publishers and graphic artists may demand expensive 24-bit color for absolute realism and accuracy, computer animators often have the luxury of being able to work on 8-bit systems. The reason for this is that computer animations, when played back on the computer rather than output to video or film, generally play at acceptable speeds only if they're played back in fast 8-bit mode. Since 24-bit images contain three times as much data, they're often just too slow to display on screen.

Remember, you can always switch a 24-bit system to display in 8-bits, so if you have a choice, choose 24.

Most Macs with built-in color offer only 8-bits. For 24-bit color, you'll usually need a color graphics board that plugs into a NuBus slot. There are too many examples of these on the market to name specific boards, though the main vendors are SuperMac, Radius, and RasterOps.

Tip:
Multimedia artists will find excellent value in QuickTime capture boards that also offer 24-bit color, video encoding, and audio capture — Radius's VideoVision and RasterOps's MediaTime, for example. While expensive, they're often a better value than adding all of these features one at a time.

Monitors are less critical than the Mac's display hardware. In general, any color monitor that works with your other hardware will be fine. One consideration for animators, however, is that larger monitors make it much easier to work on an animation while viewing lots of palettes, menus , and in the case of 3-D, several views of a scene. Because of this, some animators even use two monitors — one for their main animation screen, and the others for all the odds and ends on the Mac desktop.

Sound Sampling

Sound is another area that has greatly benefited from Apple's forging ahead with system hardware. Most Macs now have sound capture hardware built in. This is generally fine for voices and other simple sounds, but it's really not up to the task of creating high-quality sound samples for video and film animation.

The same can be said of low-cost sampling hardware that operates through the serial port. You can use Macromedia's Sound Recorder, for example, to create great voice tracks or to add simple sounds to your Mac-based presentations.

If you're aiming at the professional market with your work, you'll need to invest in additional sound capture hardware and software.

In terms of hardware, you'll need a *digital signal processor* (DSP) NuBus board. A DSP is a type of chip that specializes in converting analog information, such as audio waves, into digital information that the computer can handle. It does this at roughly ten times the speed of an ´040 processor.

Examples of audio DSP hardware include the Digidesign AudioMedia board, the RasterOps MediaTime board, and Spectral Innovations NuMedia board. These boards all allow you to record sound at audio compact disc quality or better, using your Mac's hard disk as the recording media. Another advantage of DSP boards is that they double as image processing accelerators. Programs like Photoshop and VideoFusion can use a DSP to greatly speed up the use of special effects filters and techniques like scaling and rotating images.

Scanner

A scanner is by no means mandatory for animation. However, you can achieve really cool results by scanning in images from all kinds of sources and manipulating and animating them on the Mac.

It's worth noting that many professional animators use pen and paper for sketching their storyboards and model sheets, then transfer these drawings into the Mac by scanning them. There's really no way to replace a pen and a pad of paper in terms of their feel when drawing and many animators feels they can't work without them.

Scanners can be divided into several main categories:

- **Hand scanners.** Hand scanners offer a good way for an animator on a budget to get images into the Mac. The advantages are that they're cheap (sometimes only a couple of hundred dollars), they don't require much space, and they make it easy to get small images out of hardback books, and other tough-to-get-at spots. The disadvantages are that they capture a narrow image (usually four inches wide) and they're subject to the inaccuracies of the person doing the scanning.

- **Flatbed scanners.** These are the most common, and for the animator, probably the most useful, scanners. You can draw or paint on a piece of paper (typically 8.5-by-14-inch) and scan in the result as finished artwork. There are actually two types of common flatbed scanners: grayscale, which captures everything as shades of gray, and 24-bit color, which captures everything in photorealistic color. The color flatbeds are a little more expensive than the grayscale scanners, but they offer a lot more flexibility. In general, grayscale scanners are disappearing from the market as color scanners take over.

- **Slide scanners.** These are expensive and specialized devices, usually used for publishing. The exception is a new class of low-cost 35mm scanners that handle standard negatives or slides. Nikon, Santos, and Microtech all offer versions of these. They specialize in scanning slides and negatives; the negatives being particularly cool because you can shoot a roll of film, have it developed at a 1-hour shop, and scan it immediately. If you often work from images shot with a 35mm camera, these scanners may be a good choice.

15

Video Digitizer

If your world is QuickTime, you'll have access to a cornucopia of original material if you have access to a video digitizing system such as a VideoSpigot or Movie Movie board. There are actually many such boards on the market, but these two represent the lowest-cost options.

A video capture board allows you to plug a VCR or another video output device (such as a video camera) into your Mac and capture segments of video as QuickTime movies.

While there are some SCSI video digitizers, these tend to be much slower than the NuBus board alternatives and not really much use to the QuickTime artist.

Why are some video digitizing boards so much more expensive than others? Basic boards, such as the VideoSpigot, can only capture movies at a frame size of 320-by-240 pixels (one quarter screen) under optimal conditions — and often, you have to settle for less than 30 frames per second. In general, they don't capture sound at the same time. In contrast, a system such as Radius's VideoVision Studio, incorporates a video capture board with a 24-bit display board and sound capturing hardware, it also uses a daughter board (a small board that plugs into the NuBus board) that provides hardware-assisted JPEG compression. This means you can capture a full-size video segment at a 30-frames per second. These boards are for serious multimedia people only.

Drawing Tablet

For computer drawing, the closest thing to pen and paper for computer drawing is a pressure-sensitive drawing tablet, such as those created by Wacom Inc. The tablet is a rectangular pad (popular ones for artists measure six-by-nine inches) that plugs into your Mac's serial or ADB port, depending on the model. (The ADB versions are particularly nice.) The pen looks and feels pretty much like a standard felt-tip pen. Software such as Fractal Designs Inc.'s Painter or Motion Works's Motion Paint interprets the pressure input from the pen and converts it into brush strokes or pen strokes that look very much like you're using real paints and other artists' materials.

A really unusual use of a Wacom tablet is to paint or trace over scanned-in video frames. Doing so allows you to realistically follow the line of real-life action, but create animation that looks as though it were hand-painted or drawn.

Other Stuff

Since Mac animation crosses a lot of lines, there are many odds and ends that wind up in an animator's collection. This is particularly true for professional animators.

■ **CD-ROM drive.** One of the most useful gadgets to the modern computer user is a CD-ROM drive. Vast libraries of clip art and media are available on CD. And games and multimedia, particularly those with lots of animation, are available only on CD. It won't be long before software companies only deliver their programs on CD as well.

■ **Removable storage.** If you're creating lots of animations or you need to transport animations to service bureaus for transfer to video tape, you'll need a cartridge storage system such as a Syquest or Bernoulli.

■ **Encoder.** If you're doing serious, high-end animation to video, you'll need a video encoder. This is a device that converts the RBG video signal used by your computer to an NTSC (television) signal for recording to video. These come in the form of external boxes, or as NuBus boards that fit in a slot in the Mac. Some QuickTime digitizer boards include video encoding as part of the package.

■ **Animation deck.** The least expensive, frame-accurate video animation deck is the EVO-9650 Hi-8 deck from Sony. It's about ten times the price of a good-quality standard VCR, so you'll have to really want one to go out and get it.

■ **Frame controller.** Software and NuBus boards are available for controlling animation hardware, capturing QuickTime frames at high resolution one at a time, and outputting finished animations to video one frame at a time. Since you need one or more animation decks to use a frame controller, this is a professionals-only product. The most popular Mac frame controllers are from DiaQuest Inc.

Summary

Animation hardware ranges from the most basic of Macintoshes with limited memory and disk space, to the most souped-up hot rods found on the desks of Hollywood graphics gurus.

The most important issues to consider when choosing a Mac for animation are processor speed, the amount of RAM, the size and speed of the hard disk, and the capability to work in color.

Additional tools you might consider purchasing include scanners, digitizing tablets, and specialized video recording hardware.

Hardware may go far beyond a simple computer, to include things like frame-by-frame hardware controllers, NTSC video encoders, and frame-accurate professional recording decks. However, no hardware is complete without software, and the biggest breakthrough in animation software is a system extension called QuickTime, described in the next chapter.

QuickTime

QuickTime is one of the most important developments in computer animation. Simply put, it's software that provides a fast, efficient, and easy way to work with movies and sounds on your Mac. (Both QuickTime and Apple's Movie Player application are included on the *Cool Animation Disk*.)

QuickTime is system software that handles the high-speed compression, decompression, and synchronization of digital media. This means you can work with video, sounds, still pictures, and animations much more efficiently and effectively than ever before.

Almost any Mac can run QuickTime, although it's recommended you have System 7 installed for a bunch of reasons. The software itself is a single extension that's installed in the

Extensions folder in your System Folder. When you reboot your Mac, QuickTime is automatically available to any software that can take advantage of it. Think of QuickTime as a VCR for your Mac. Programs like Flo', PROmotion, and editing and special effects software like Video Fusion, QuickFlix, and AVID Sparrow can all automatically record and play back animations and video using QuickTime.

Macs with a 68020 processor or better can run QuickTime as long as they have enough RAM. Older Macs, such as the SE, Plus, and Classic, may or may not be able to run QuickTime, depending on whether they've been upgraded, the amount of RAM, and the version of system software they're running. In general, since they lack color and speed, we don't recommend them for use with QuickTime.

Perhaps the most interesting element of QuickTime is that it has blurred the distinction between *digital* and *analog* media. Music, video, and pictures, such as those that make up an animation, are traditionally analog information. Analog information comes in "waves," in the case of sounds, or "continuous tones," in the case of pictures. But a computer works only in the digital world. Digital information travels in *bits,* or small, discrete pieces—instead of smooth, continuous brush strokes, you get many small bits or pixels that combine to look like a brush stroke.

Getting analog pictures, such as video or still photographs, into the computer requires a process called *digitizing.* For still images, digitizing is accomplished with a *scanner.* Scanners include hand scanners, flatbed scanners, and slide scanners, which all accomplish the same task using slightly different techniques. Video digitizing requires special hardware inside your Mac (some of the latest Mac models have built-in video digitizing hardware). Common examples of video digitizing hardware include SuperMac's VideoSpigot, Radius Inc.'s VideoVision, and RasterOps's MediaTime board.

Converting analog information into digital information and back is not particularly difficult from a computer programmer's perspective. The problem is the sheer amount of information being delivered. Consider a single frame of an animation. An image that fills a video screen is 640 pixels wide by 480 pixels high, or 307,200 total pixels. To further complicate things, a color image maintains red, green, and blue information for each pixel, thereby tripling the amount of data required, so that single image is now equal to 921,600 individual "bytes" of data. (In case you really trip on this number stuff, each byte is made up of 8 "bits," allowing it to contain a color number from 0 to 255. That value is the intensity level of the red, green, or blue value of the specific pixel. Incidentally, eight bits multiplied by three channels adds up to 24-bit color.) In some animations, an "alpha channel" is also stored with RGB values, bumping the image up to 32 bits of information; this is the limit under the Mac's 32-bit operating system. We'll return to the alpha channel later.

In terms even the most out-of-date computer geeks can handle, all this means is that a single frame of an animation, in its native state, takes up almost 1M of memory and disk space. Consider that a typical animation or video has 24 or 30 frames per second (fps), and you can see that the situation quickly gets out of hand—even with an 80M or 100M hard disk and lots of RAM. Essentially, there are two problems. First, since it takes time to store and retrieve data from a hard disk (3M per second is considered a fast disk) it's impossible to get data off the drive fast enough to play back an animation at a convincing rate. Secondly, nobody has that much disk space. Even at 15 fps, a single 30-second movie might require 500M of space!

Impressive Compression

A most excellent solution to this most woeful of conditions is to make the movies smaller through a technique called *compression*. QuickTime is the software that makes this happen.

I can tell that you are thinking, "Chill for a second! How do you *compress* something that's nothing but bits and bytes of electromagnetism in the first place?"

Compression is a technique used by programmers to make files take up less space on a disk. They do this by throwing away surplus information when a file is being stored on a disk, and then recreating that information when the file is opened again. QuickTime uses "lossy" compression, which means that what you gain by compressing your animation, you pay for with the loss of some information from your animation (i.e., the loss of some image quality).

QuickTime only saves the *changes* from one frame to the next. In a typical animation, for example, the background may remain unchanged for the first 100 frames. In this case, the background pixels are saved only once. Meanwhile, the foreground characters may jump around on the screen, change color, and otherwise metamorphose into strange and wonderful visions. The pixels that change during the animation are saved whenever they change.

Video Versus Animation

What's the difference between video and animation? There isn't one, really. You can create animations that act like video or digitize video of animations. On the computer, the distinction between them is lost since everything becomes a digital image and plays by the same rules. The only important distinction, from a computer animator's point of view, is that video generally contains more complex images, such as those taken of natural scenes with a camera while animations generally use simplified pictures, such as line drawings.

In typical live video the background is moving, the foreground is moving, and all kinds of other stuff is going on, pretty much every pixel in every frame is different from the previous frame. In an animation, on the other hand, you'll often have only a few lines and simple shapes that change from frame-to-frame while the background changes only slightly or not at all. Fortunately, QuickTime deals with the differences between animations and video by offering different *compressors* (see figure 3.1).

Figure 3.1
QuickTime
compression settings

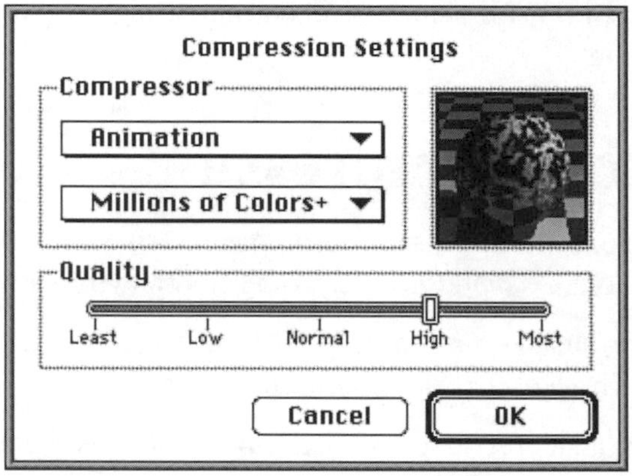

Video Compressor

The Video compressor makes some generalizations about blocks of pixels, averaging small blocks into regions of a single color. The result is video which plays back acceptably, as long as you don't mind some compression *artifacts*, or weird-looking, but subtle glitches that weren't present in the original. QuickTime is capable of a wide range of compression—anywhere from a 2-to-1 ratio all the way down to 30-to-1. The trade-off is playback speed versus image quality. At very low levels of compression, such as 2-to-1, QuickTime will save every minute change made to every frame. At higher levels, the software becomes less discriminating, saving only significant changes to 20-pixel-square blocks, for example.

Animation Compressor

The Animation compressor understands that you want to save every change in every frame, so instead of compressing block-by-block, it saves only changes in individual pixels from frame-to-frame. If you try this with complex video, you'll get poor compression and rotten playback rates. However, if you use it with a typical animation, the compression and playback will far exceed what you normally expect from your Mac. Yahoo!

Another important benefit of the Animation compressor is that at the **Millions+** color setting, this compressor retains an animation's *alpha channel*. This is sometimes known as a *mask*, and it's used by sophisticated software to seamlessly composite multiple layers of graphics, such as an animated character over a background (see figure 3.2).

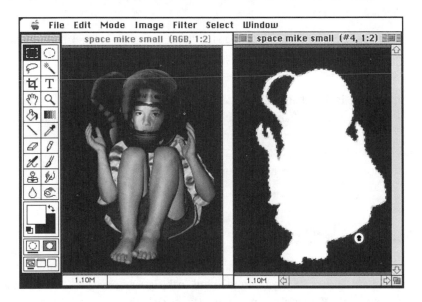

Figure 3.2

An image and its alpha channel

The alpha channel is a separate image, carried along with the normal image, that defines transparency, like a stencil. Where the alpha channel is white, you can see the image, where it's black, the background shows through. When you're working with animations, the alpha channel is really powerful: you could, for example, have animated titles scroll across a background movie, with another, different movie playing inside the shapes of the titles.

Other Compressors

In addition to video and animation, there are many other QuickTime compressors that are well-suited to different tasks.

- **Cinepak.** This compressor, from Apple, is used to maximize playback speeds when playing video directly from the Mac. It gives you performance roughly twice that of the Video compressor. One catch, however, is that it takes about 10 times as long to compress the movie in the first place.

- ■ **Photo-JPEG.** This is primarily used for compressing still images, such as scanned photographs. It's very efficient, and it maintains image quality as much as possible, but it's too slow for use with movies.

- ■ **Graphics.** Similar to an Animation compressor, this preserves an image's quality as much as possible.

- ■ **Custom.** These compressors go by many different names, and they're developed to work with a specific piece of custom hardware, such as Radius's VideoVision or SuperMac's Digital Film.

The bottom line is that thanks to QuickTime compression, it's possible to play back animations at an acceptable frame rate. (Test your math skills: If your hard disk delivers data at 3M per second and you need to play back your animation of 1M frames at 24 frames per second, what kind of compression will you need? The answer is: You'll need at least an 8-to-1 compression ratio to squeeze it all through.)

Sound Decisions

Next to compression, QuickTime's coolest contribution is the synchronization of different kinds of media, particularly animation and sound. In the past when you created animations on the computer, the Mac would do its best to play back whatever material it was supposed to, usually with sick results. The reason for this, as we've already mentioned, is that getting lots of frames of an animation through the computer is a formidable task; add digitized sound to an already stuffed-to-the-gills data path, and your Mac is likely to come up choking and gasping for air. Images may crawl onto the screen while sound plays at slow-record speeds, or the sound may fail to play at all. QuickTime astutely compromises by assuming that the smooth playback of sound takes precedence over the quick presentation of an animation's frames. (Try listening to music while flipping the sound on and off—it sounds crummy. On the other hand, try flipping through this book slowly and occasionally skip pages—even though the animation is jumpy, it maintains an acceptable sense of flow.)

When you play back a QuickTime movie that has a sound track, QuickTime will keep the sound playing smoothly. If the system begins to bog down on excess data, it will *drop frames* from the animation, resulting in glitches in the animation's motion. The faster your Mac, the fewer the dropped frames and the smoother the motion.

Direct Delivery

Without QuickTime, computer animators had to copy their images one-frame-at-a-time to video or film using expensive, specialized recording hardware. The resulting video or film was then played using standard video hardware or projectors. With QuickTime, even low-budget, but totally cool, animators like you can make the most of what the Mac can do.

Copy and Paste

QuickTime has one other crucial benefit. In the past, it was difficult for programmers to create software that would efficiently save and play back animations, and each program used its own method (usually one that was incompatible with that used by other programs). That meant that while you could create an animation, you couldn't copy and paste it into another program. As everyone knows, cutting and pasting is what the Mac's all about.

Now, with the help of QuickTime, scores of new programs are popping up that let you do all kinds of strange and excellent things that qualify as animation. And animations you create in one program can be easily moved into and further tweaked in another. Flo', the most righteous program that's included on the *Cool Animation Disk*, is a happy example of one of these programs. In fact, just about every program that ever had anything to do with Mac animation is now QuickTime compatible. This means that if you can create an animation, you can save it as a QuickTime movie, and if your program can play animations, it can almost certainly play QuickTime movies. Even some word processors allow you to place QuickTime movies in them.

QuickTime Installation

The *Cool Animation Disk* includes the current version of QuickTime. There is a very good chance that you already have it if your Mac's new, but if you don't, here's how you get it to work:

1. Put the *Cool Animation Disk* in the floppy drive and open it.

2. Double-click on the "QuickTime stuff.sea" icon.

3. Specify the hard disk to which you want QuickTime Stuff copied.

4. Once you've unstuffed the archive on the floppy to your hard disk, open your hard disk and note that there are two new files enclosed. The first one, "Movie Player," is the application that lets you play back—and even edit—QuickTime movies. Leave that one alone for now.

5. The item of interest is called "QuickTime." Locate the System Folder on your hard disk and drag the QuickTime icon onto it. You should get a message that looks like figure 3.3.

Figure 3.3

QuickTime install screen

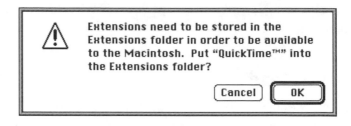

> ⚠ **Extensions need to be stored in the Extensions folder in order to be available to the Macintosh. Put "QuickTime™" into the Extensions folder?**
>
> [Cancel] [OK]

6. Click OK.

7. Now double-click the "Cool Mac Animation.sea" file.

8. When you get the dialog box, choose your hard drive and click on OK.

9. Once the Mac's finished copying, choose **Restart** from the **Special** menu. Now you have a folder called "Cool Mac Animation" on your hard drive. You'll need it in chpater 5.

If you happen to be running System 6, you'll need the System 6 QuickTime patch, available from Hayden's online forum. See chapter 9, "Downloading Software," for further instructions.

QuickTime Alternatives

QuickTime is not the only compression and playback software available. People were doing similar things prior to Apple's entry into the animation market. Two file formats maintain particular importance, partly because not everybody has caught up to the QuickTime generation, and partly because they address some needs that QuickTime neglects.

Numbered PICT

PICT is the standard still image format for the Mac, and is supported almost universally by Mac graphics software. For this reason, it's also a fairly common format used by animators, particularly those whose creations will eventually end up on video or film. Animators generally use a special system for saving animations as PICT files, *numbered PICT*. The files

themselves are no different than standard PICT files, which means any graphics software can open them. The only difference is that the files are usually named when saving, then automatically appended with a sequential number, such as "Rosebud movie 0001"; "Rosebud movie 0002"; "Rosebud movie 0003"; and so on.

Numbered PICT is a non-compression format. Frames are simply saved as individual PICTs. The advantage of this is that quality is absolutely preserved. Although these individual frames may be very large, you can bring them into a painting or image editing program one at a time for retouching or rotoscoping, something you can't necessarily do with animation file formats.

PICS

PICS is a file format originally introduced by VIDI, a company that makes expensive, powerful 3-D graphics software for the Mac. PICS originally provided a method for designers to show people their 3-D animations without having to record their animations to tape. More importantly, it allowed you to save all of the frames of an animation in a single file. This was much more convenient than keeping folders full of hundreds of numbered images. Finally, VIDI offered a player that could open these files and play them back as fast as the Mac would allow.

Vendors quickly caught on to this format, in particular, Macromedia Inc. (it was MacroMind at the time). MacroMind Director, a high-end program for creating animations, seized on PICS as a way to store its own animations so that other programs could use them. Soon, many vendors offered PICS support for their software products.

Eventually, it became clear that PICS needed some kind of compression system. Some programs began to allow frame differencing compression, along the lines of QuickTime's current Animation compressor. PICS offered (and still does) some of the basic features of QuickTime, but lacks much of QuickTime's sophistication.

The biggest difference between PICS and QuickTime is that PICS is simply a method for storing multiple frames. QuickTime goes far beyond this in that it is time-based. No matter how difficult an animation is to play, nor how slow your computer, QuickTime will play it in the specified time and in synch (if it can't, it simply won't play at all). Programs that use PICS, in contrast, will simply play every frame, no matter how long it takes.

Another limitation of PICS is that it offers no memory management. QuickTime is optimized for streaming huge files from disk, but PICS requires that the whole animation be loaded into RAM prior to playback.

Currently, the best reason to use PICS is that thousands of clip animations are available in this format. Online services, including America Online and CompuServe, feature bulletin boards with all kinds of cool clips you can use in your own projects. Commercial clip providers are quickly upgrading everything to QuickTime format, however.

A few outdated programs are still well adapted to work with PICS, but not with QuickTime. Fortunately, most QuickTime editors—programs designed for editing and adding effects to QuickTime movies—can automatically convert a PICS file into a QuickTime movie.

Re-Animator

A program called Re-Animator, written by Russ LaValle, is available free from online services, including CompuServe (see chapter 9, "Downloading Software").

This tiny program has a single, simple function—to play PICS files. Because the program is only 18K, you can easily put a large animation PICS with it on a single floppy disk and send it to your friends. It's not nearly as cool or sophisticated as the QuickTime approach, but it will get you by in a pinch, especially if you have a Mac without enough RAM to run QuickTime.

When you launch Re-Animator, instructions appear onscreen explaining how to load a PICS file and set the speed for playback. It's really very simple to use.

PACo Is One Cool Joe

A company called CoSA (Company of Science & Art, now a division of Aldus Corp.) offers a great product called "PACo Producer." Like QuickTime, PACo is a time-based compression and playback system. It was actually available well before Apple shipped QuickTime, but it only caught on in small numbers.

The reason savvy animators and multimedia producers still use it is that there are versions for a whole bunch of different computers. If you have PACo running on an IBM PC or a SPARCstation, for example, you can open and play a PACo animation created on a Mac. PACo's playback is extremely fast, in some cases even better than QuickTime—which is another reason to consider using it. The final big feature of PACo is that you can get a special CD-ROM from CoSA that allows you to simulate performance of your own multimedia project as if it were playing off a CD-ROM drive, *before* you endure the massive expense of mastering a CD. Needless to say, this is mostly important to high-end power users creating professional animations for distribution on CD.

While the cross platform capabilities of PACo are really cool—QuickTime is limited to Mac and Windows—it doesn't enjoy anywhere near the support that QuickTime does. In fact, the only way to create a PACo animation on the Mac is to save your animation as PICS, numbered PICTs, or QuickTime and then open and recompress them with PACo producer.

Summary

QuickTime is the most important event in making Mac animation accessible to the average user. It is system software that enables your Mac to work with and play back animations and sounds while maintaining synchronization between these elements, regardless of the Mac's power.

QuickTime provides compression and decompression of images and sounds, reducing the amount of storage space they require, and increasing the speed with which you can play them from your Mac's hard disk.

Because different animators and graphic artists work with different kinds of images, QuickTime offers many different types of compressors, such as Video, Animation, and JPEG. For animators, the Animation compressor is possibly the most useful, particularly because it supports alpha channel transparency.

QuickTime is only the latest and coolest method of storing animation files. Other methods included PICS, numbered PICT, and PACo Producer.

While there are specialized options, the coolest killer animation software is almost sure to require QuickTime, or at least work with it in wonderous ways. Read chapter 4, "Killer Animation Software," to learn more.

Killer Animation Software

There are really several different kinds of animation software available for the Mac. They can be broken down into several major categories:

- **Cel animation.** Used for creating traditional Disney-style hand-painted frame-by-frame animations. These packages specialize in 2-D characters animated over paths.

- **Morphing and warping.** This software gives you god privileges over digital pictures. You can mold and transform images at will.

- **3-D animation.** Software that mimics the three-dimensional world. Build models, add textures and lights, and generate rendered animations in perspective.

■ **Editing and special effects.** These aren't really animation programs at all—but QuickTime editors that allow you to combine, edit, and add sounds and special effects to your animated creations.

In this chapter, we'll concentrate on cel animation software. The following chapters deal with other three.

Cel animation software makes traditional-style animation easy. Programs like PROmotion and Animation Works are specifically designed to do cel animation, complete with onion-skinning, tweening, cycling, layering, and other tricks of the traditional animator's trade. Of course, they also add many tools and capabilities not available to the traditional animator, such as the creation of interactive multimedia, path animation, and other special features.

Among the coolest cel animation programs are: ADDmotion II and Motion Paint from Motion Works Inc.; PROmotion; Gold Disk's Animation Works; and Vividus's Cinemation. All of these programs can be purchased for under $200; they're also sometimes bundled with other software packages.

ADDmotion II

Motion Works Inc.
524 Second Street
San Francisco, CA 94107
Phone: (415) 541-9333
Fax: (415) 541-0555

List price: $99 (may be available bundled with HyperCard 2.2)

System requirements: HyperCard 2.1 or later, System 6.0.7 or System 7. For black-and-white, 2M of RAM, 4M for color (in addition to system requirements).

ADDmotion II (see figure 4.1), from Motion Works, is one of the hottest cel animation programs available for the Mac. In the first place, it can be used to create animated multimedia productions, complete with sounds, buttons, and interactivity. But ADDmotion's coolest feature is its strong set of tools for creating animations and to save as QuickTime movies or PICS files.

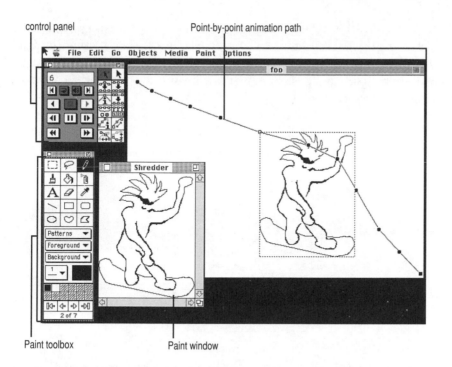

control panel — Point-by-point animation path

Paint toolbox — Paint window

Figure 4.1
ADDmotion's main screen

ADDmotion II is tightly integrated with HyperCard. In the days when HyperCard was black-and-white only, ADDmotion II was one of the only (and best) ways to add color to HyperCard stacks. Apple chose to bundle the two of them when it shipped HyperCard 2.2, its colorized version, at the end of 1993. (HyperCard was colorized largely though extensions originally created for ADDmotion.)

When you install ADDmotion II to HyperCard, it is automatically added to your Home Stack. The Home Stack will include a button that lets you turn the ADDmotion resources on or off. If you are at all familiar with HyperCard programming, you'll find it easy to work with ADDmotion to create interactive animations.

ADDmotion II is a cel animator that relies partly on traditional techniques, but it also contains path animation tools, tweening, and other animation automation tools. This means you can create a *sprite* (also called an *actor* or *character*) made up of multiple cels, such as a monster running, then animate the sprite by dragging it around the screen. ADDmotion automatically moves the monster across the screen as its legs move, its arms flail, and fire shoots from its toothsome jaws.

The tools for using ADDmotion are really very simple once you get the hang of them. A 24-bit paint program is integrated with a cel sequencer and an onion-skinning feature (see figure 4.2). As you draw new cels for your animation, a dimmed version of your next (or previous) frame appears in your drawing window. This makes it easy to trace over cels and to modify them slightly from frame-to-frame.

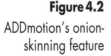

Figure 4.2

ADDmotion's onion-skinning feature

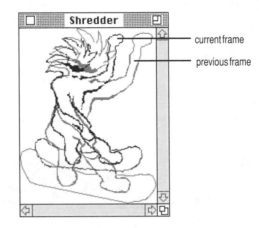

current frame

previous frame

If you have access to digitized video saved as PICS files, you can import a series of frames as a character, insert blank cels in between the digitized frames, and use the onion-skinning feature to trace over the video frames. This means you don't have to be a master of hand-eye coordination to draw and animate cool characters. You can use the forms of real people and creatures as a starting point. In general, this is a technique you can employ whenever you're doing Mac graphics—it's a great way for a creative, but not gifted, person to create cool digital artwork.

Creating After Dark Modules

ADDmotion can save its movies as stand-alone players that you can run by double-clicking an icon; it can also save QuickTime movies, PICS files, and even screen saver modules for use in Berkeley System's After Dark. You can drive your friends insane with envy by creating screen savers featuring cartoon characters you've invented yourself.

Just Add Motion

The animation interface in ADDmotion is divided into several key components: the Paint module that, as we've mentioned, has standard painting tools, plus a cel navigator that allows

you to quickly switch among a character's individual frames; a sound editor, that allows you to easily record and edit the sound track for your movie; and Action, that contains ADDmotion's path animation tools and also controls interactivity. The TimeLines window (see figure 4.3) controls the layering and duration of characters and backdrops.

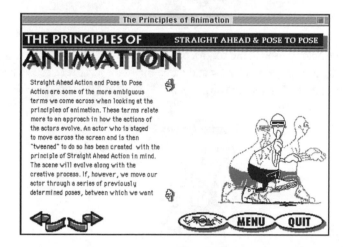

Figure 4.3
ADDmotion's Action module

Getting Started

ADDmotion II comes with the best interactive animation tutorial we've ever seen (see figure 4.4). It's a HyperCard stack called "Principles of Animation," and it goes a long way toward teaching a new animator some of the most important concepts of animation: squash and stretch, anticipation, secondary action, straight ahead versus pose-to-pose action, follow through and overlapping action, slow in and slow out, arcs of motion, staging, timing, exaggeration, solid drawing, and character appeal.

Figure 4.4
Addmotion's "The Principles of Animation" stack

A really unique feature of ADDmotion is its support of HyperCard events. This allows you to launch ADDmotion animations using HyperCard buttons; conversely, you can have interactive ADDmotion animations that trigger HyperCard messages or events.

Creating an ADDmotion Animation

1. To create a new animation in ADDmotion, begin by creating a new stack and saving it as My First Animation. Then choose **New Animation** from the **File** menu and call the animation Water Drops; this will automatically open the Paint window.

2. Begin by drawing a new background prop using the standard paint tools. (You add new colors to the palette by selecting the Foreground pull-down menu and picking one). In this case, draw a water faucet (see figure 4.5). Once the drawing is complete, click the close box and save the new prop as Faucet at the prompt.

Figure 4.5

Faucet, ready to drip

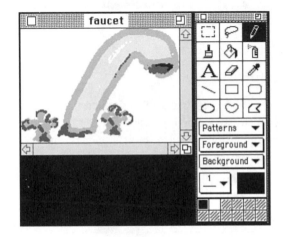

3. Click the Actor button in the control panel (see figure 4.6). A dialog box will ask you for an actor to place. Click New and name the Actor Droplet. The character paint window and the Paint toolbox will open.

Figure 4.6

ADDmotion's control panel

Actor button

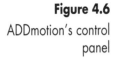

4. Paint the first stage of a water droplet forming (see figure 4.7).

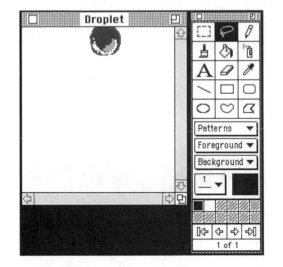

Figure 4.7
Water droplet, stage 1

5. Choose **Insert Cels...** from the **Edit** menu, and in the Insert Cels... dialog box (see figure 4.8), enter 5 in the Number of Cels to Insert box. Leave the Duplicate Cel Contents checkbox unchecked. Click OK; now you should see a blank cel (see figure 4.9). The Cel Controller at the bottom of the Paint toolbox shows the message "2 of 6." This means that you are working on an actor that contains six cels, five of which are blank (you're currently in cel 2).

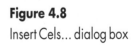

Figure 4.8
Insert Cels... dialog box

37

Figure 4.9
Cel 2 is blank

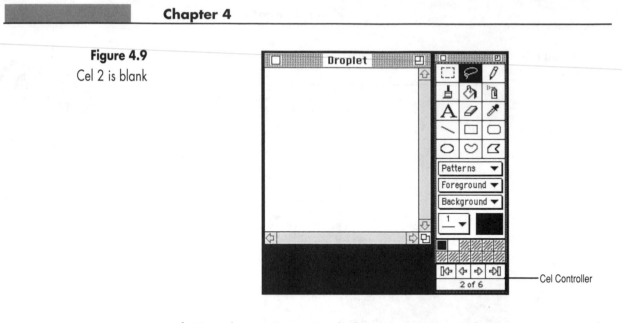

Cel Controller

6. Go to the **Options** menu and select **Onion Skin**. Now, choose **Previous Cel**. A dim version of your first frame appears in the drawing window (see figure 4.10).

Figure 4.10
Cel 2 blank, but
showing dimmed
version of cel 1

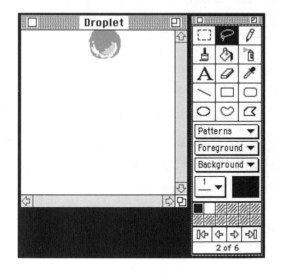

7. Trace over the dimmed droplet, modifying it slightly to make it larger than the first (see figure 4.11).

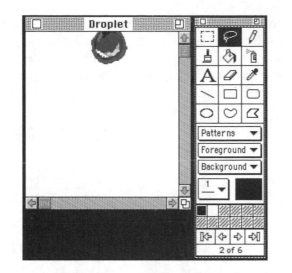

Figure 4.11
Droplet, traced over

8. Click on the Forward Arrow in the Cel Controller in the Paint toolbox to go to cel 3 (see figure 4.12). The droplet you just drew appears, in a dimmed form, in the drawing window. Repeat the step-and-trace procedure until you have enough cels to make a realistic droplet. Switch off onion-skinning occasionally to see the cels without the ghosted image of the previous frame.

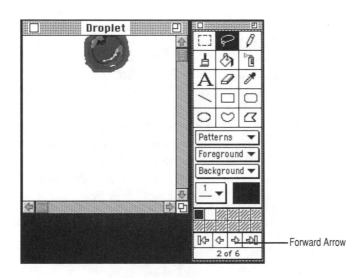

Forward Arrow

Figure 4.12
The final "droplet" cel

9. Be sure to increase the size and downward stretch of each subsequent cel slightly (see figure 4.13). In this animation, we've actually created twenty-six cels to create a very smooth elaborate animation (note the number in the cel counter) where the droplets shatter upon impact. You'll find that work goes very quickly once you get started, although six cels or so is often enough to create a convincing sprite.

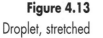

Figure 4.13

Droplet, stretched

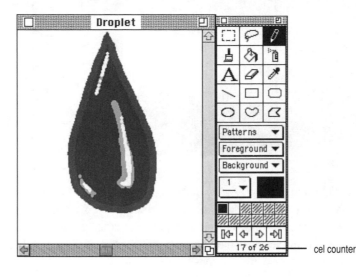

cel counter

Note:

One of the most important principles of cool animations is to give characters a sense of weight and volume. Things that ripple, squeeze, stretch, ooze, and undulate are much more lifelike than smoothly flowing stick figures. These effects give *weight* to an object, which is crucial to natural motion.

10. Once you've finished a series of cels, use the Cel Controller at the bottom of the Paint palette to step backward through your completed cels. (Note that it cycles all the way around until you come back to where you started.) Use this to smooth and refine the motion of your cels until you've finished a complete "drop plop."

11. A cool trick is to press the mouse on the forward key and hold it; this plays back the animated water droplet at full speed so you can see how it will look when played back.

Note:

Alternating between one-frame-at-a-time and full-speed playback is the best way to work out the motion of characters and eradicate the little glitches that can detract from their flow. The need to do this constantly is one of the most compelling reasons for traditional animators to use computers: without them, an animator has to put everything on film before he can see what he's made.

12. Set the registration for each of the cels. In this case, were going to set the registration at the top vertical point of each cel and in the horizontal center (the point where a water droplet clings to a faucet before dropping). To set the registration point, check the Registration option in the **Options** menu. Choose **Objects/Get Info...**, to open the character in a preview window (showing the cel relative to the size of the screen), with a pair of cross hairs intersecting at the cel's registration point (see figure 4.14). You simply drag these cross hairs to reposition them.

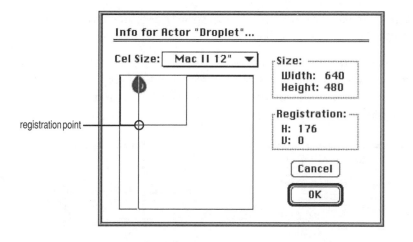

registration point —

Figure 4.14
The Info dialog for the Droplet sprite

13. Click the close box. The sprite now appears somewhere on the main animation screen. Click the Rewind button (see figure 4.15) on the control panel to go to the first frame of the animation and drag the Droplet character to the lip of the faucet.

Figure 4.15

A drippy faucet

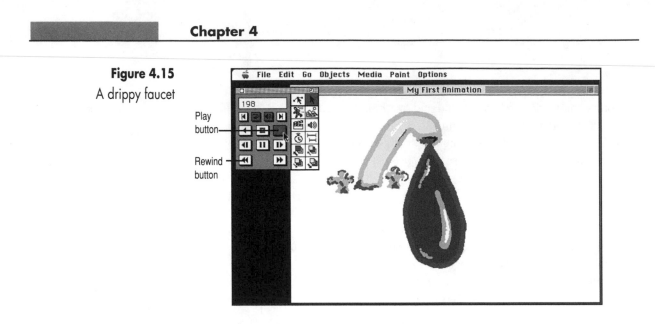

14. Click the Play button on the animation control panel (see figure 4.15). The animated sprite plays back in its new location.

15. In this example, the Droplet character is 26 cels. Choose the **Objects/Info** menu to bring up the Actor Information... dialog box (see figure 4.16), set the duration of the Droplet character to last only from frame 1 to 25, otherwise, it will cycle over and over again throughout the length of the movie.

Figure 4.16

Actor information

16. Use the **Media** menu to select **Animation Options...** (see figure 4.17) to set the movie duration to 100 frames. This will create a suspenseful pause between each droplet as the animation loops around. Also in this dialog, change the frame rate to 30 frames per second.

```
┌──────────────────────────────────────────────────────┐
│  Animation Options...                                  │
│  ────────────────────────────────────────────         │
│  Animation Name: │Water Drops                    │     │
│  ┌Contains:─────────────┐   ☐ Hide Palettes             │
│  │ Actors:   1          │   ☐ Hide Menu Bar             │
│  │ Props:    1          │   ☐ Hide Cursor               │
│  │ Sounds:   0          │   ☒ Auto Replay               │
│  │ Cues:     0          │   ☐ Mouse Button to Stop       │
│  │ Events:   0          │   ☒ Command-(.) to Stop        │
│  └──────────────────────┘   ☒ Show Frame Count          │
│  Frames:    │100│           ☐ Show Frame Rate           │
│  Speed:     │ 30  ▼│        ☐ Leave Last Frame          │
│  FF/REW Skip: │5│ ▲▼        ☐ Preserve Image            │
│                             ☐ Multifinder Animation     │
│  Grid Size:  │OFF ▼│        ☐ Allow Card Clicks         │
│  Background Color │   │   ( Cancel )  ▐ OK ▌            │
└──────────────────────────────────────────────────────┘
```

frames per second

Figure 4.17
Animation Options... dialog box

17. Finally, add sound effects. To do this, simply move to a frame in the animation where you want the sound to begin playing. Click on the Sound button in the Control Panel, and then use the Sound Information dialog box to locate a sound file. When you have want you want, click OK. In our example, we'll use a water droplet sound that plays at the twenty-first frame (at which the droplet strikes the ground). If you don't have a water droplet sound, consider a "quack" or some other sound.

Figure 4.18

Sound information
dialog

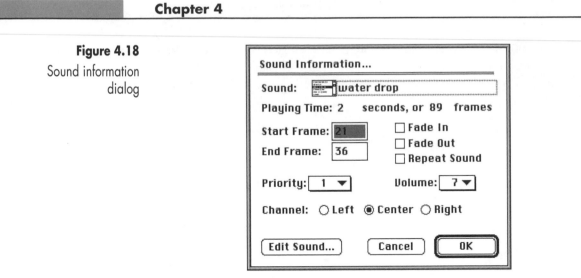

18. ADDmotion also lets you add cool effects to sounds (see figure 4.19). (Click on the Edit Sound... button in the Sound Information... dialog box to do this.)

Figure 4.19

Editing sound

19. Now, play back your cool, drippy, new animation! (Use the play button in the control panel.)

While it's possible to get far more sophisticated with ADDmotion, this example should give you a good idea of how easy it is to work with this program.

44

Interactivity

ADDmotion lets you add interactive buttons to animated screens. These, in turn, can do just about anything a standard HyperCard button can do (which is just about anything you can imagine doing with a computer, since HyperCard allows full-blown programming).

At the same time, HyperCard stacks can include ADDmotion animations that can be controlled directly by HyperCard. For example, you might create a card with a menu of buttons, so that each button launches a different animation. Because HyperCard is such a powerful multimedia tool, using ADDmotion with HyperCard gives you almost unlimited flexibility for combining animation with other multimedia activities.

Additionally, you can distribute run-time versions of animations you create within HyperCard free-of-charge. Thus, you can create HyperCard stacks with lots of cool self-playing animations and distribute them just like any other stacks you create. For the HyperCard programmer and multimedia artist, there's no other program like it.

PROmotion

Motion Works Inc.
524 Second Street
San Francisco, CA 94107
Phone: (415) 541-9333
Fax: (415) 541-0555

List price: call Motion Works.

System requirements: System 6.0.7 or System 7. For black-and-white, 2M of RAM, 4M for color (in addition to system requirements).

PROmotion, also from Motion Works, is another great cel animation program for the Mac (see figure 4.20). Unfortunately, as this book went to press, the program was in a strange no-man's land: Motion Works licensed the code for the program to Corel Systems, but stopped marketing the program itself (although you may still be able to get it by calling Motion Works). Corel used the Windows version of PROmotion to add animation tools (called Corel Move) to its best-selling Windows program, Corel Draw. It is supposed to do the same thing to Corel Draw for the Mac, only Corel Draw Mac was still only a gleam in Corel's eye as of December, 1993. If Corel Draw Mac ships in 1994, it will almost certainly include a version of PROmotion renamed Corel Move.

Figure 4.20

PROmotion main
screen

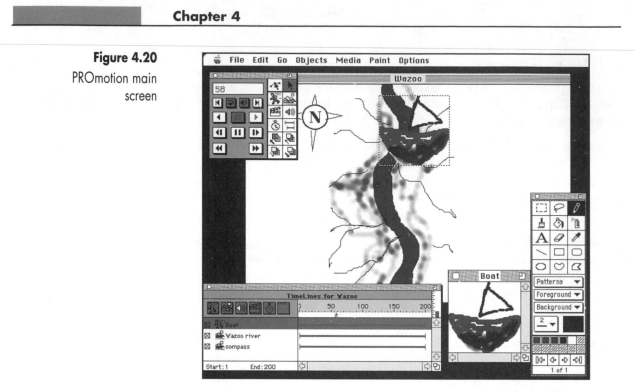

So what is PROmotion? Get this: It's identical to the first version of ADDmotion II in all but a few respects. In the first place, it can be used to create animated multimedia productions, complete with sounds, buttons, and interactivity. But unlike ADDmotion II, it doesn't require HyperCard. It's a completely stand-alone animation application. PROmotion's interface is virtually identical to ADDmotion's. Like ADDmotion, it can save animations as QuickTime movies or PICS files; or it can save them as After Dark modules and stand-alone run-time players. While PROmotion doesn't have a direct interface to HyperCard, it offers send-and-receive support for AppleEvents. Programs that support AppleEvents can control PROmotion animations, and vice versa.

While the features of PROmotion are identical to those of ADDmotion II, it seems likely that it will quickly become outdated as Motion Works turns its attention elsewhere. Currently, Motion Works plans to add a number of features to ADDmotion II that aren't found in PROmotion, such as support for pressure-sensitive tablets.

(A working demo version of PROmotion is available on the CompuServe Hayden forum. See chapter 9, "Downloading Software," for an explanation of how to download it.)

PROmotion also supports Publish and Subscribe, so you can subscribe to a drawing you've created in a painting program (for example, Painter) and your PROmotion character, the *subscriber*, will be automatically updated if you make changes to your drawing in the paint

46

program. This allows you to use any really cool paint or drawing program that supports Publish and Subscribe, instead of PROmotion's somewhat simplistic painting module. The disadvantage of this technique is that you can't use it with PROmotion's onion-skinning feature. If you are lucky enough to own Painter, its tracing feature can be used like the onion-skinning feature of PROmotion, although it's not as easy to use.

MotionPaint

Motion Works Inc.
524 Second Street
San Francisco, CA 94107
Phone: (415) 541-0555

List price: $249 (bundled with the Motion Works Utilities)

System requirements: Not available at press time.

This program hadn't shipped as of late 1993, but here's what Motion Works says it will do: basically, MotionPaint is the painting and cel animating part of ADDmotion II, spruced up with features like support for pressure-sensitive drawing tablets, but without the interactive presentation and path animation tools.

Much more importantly, however, MotionPaint will allow you to import a PICS or a QuickTime movie, and individually paint on any frame.

This provides a smooth, custom interface for rotoscoping video or creating animations. Tools like onion-skinning and registration ensure that everything will line up and flow smoothly.

This program is probably the centerpiece of the Motion Works Utilities, and if it lives up to the promise of early previews, it will be a must-have for any animator.

Cinemation

Vividus Corp.
651 Kendall Avenue
Palo Alto, CA 94306
Phone: (415) 494-2111
Fax: (415) 492-2221

List price: $495; $245 for CD-only version.

System requirements: 2M RAM for color, 1M for black-and-white (in addition to system requirements). System 6.0.7 or later. System 7 users need version 7.1. You can also play movies within HyperCard if you have version 2.0 or later.

Cinemation is a sophisticated cel animation program, that has lots of features for giving onscreen presentations. It's actually available in two formats: a low-cost CD-ROM edition, and the regular floppy-disk version. While the floppy version is considerably more expensive than the other cel-based animation programs mentioned in this chapter, the CD-ROM edition is just about the same price as the others.

A demo version of Cinemation is available in the Hayden online forum. (See chapter 9, "Downloading Software," for instructions on how to obtain a copy.)

Cinemation is mostly geared toward path-based animation. It has a simple-to-use VCR-style control panel (see figure 4.21) for animating objects that lets you simply click Record, then drag an object across the screen to record its motion.

Figure 4.21

Cinemation main screen

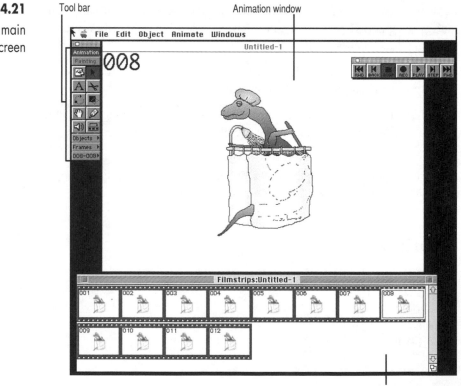

Tool bar

Animation window

cel editing window

48

Like most cel animators, Cinemation is a frame-based, rather than a time-based animation program; this means that every event is synchronized to a particular frame and that it will play every frame of the animation without keeping synch with time-based media such as QuickTime. It will, however, export animations as QuickTime movies and also let you place QuickTime movies in an animation (you have to insert an interactive "Pause" to allow an embedded QuickTime movie to play to the end).

As with ADDmotion II and Corel Move, it's very easy to add simple interactivity (see figure 4.22) to Cinemation using onscreen buttons that jump to other locations in an animation. One of the business-oriented aspects of Cinemation is that you can import a PowerPoint or Persuasion presentation and automatically add animation to parts of the presentation.

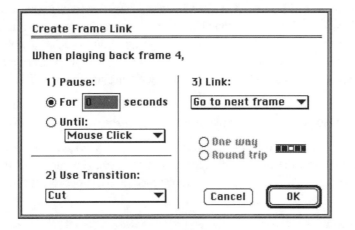

Figure 4.22

Creating interactivity in Cinemation

The program also has a full-featured cel animation mode (it uses a filmstrip metaphor). You can select any frame in a film strip to bring it into the paint window. Using the Ghosting feature, you can do onion-skinning of sequential frames. You can even select a range of frames to onion-skin simultaneously, which is sometimes helpful for getting smooth-flowing motion. Like all good cel animators, it includes a registration tool for getting your characters to line up properly.

Cinemation features a full 24-bit paint program that works with the Ghosting feature. But you can also import PICT files into a single frame of a character, or import PICS files to fill a range of cells.

Like most up-to-date multimedia programs, Cinemation lets you import or record your own sounds (see figure 4.23).

Figure 4.23

Cinemation sound
dialog box

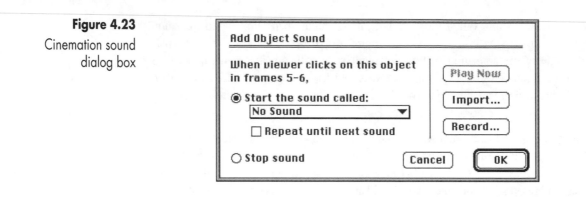

Cinemation comes with a HyperCard XCMD which allows you to play your animations in HyperCard stacks. When you install this XCMD in HyperCard, HyperCard buttons can be used to jump to a frame of an animation, activate a sound or a link attached to a named object in the movie, or even replace animated text in a movie with new text from a HyperCard message. Clicking on objects in a movie can also send messages to HyperCard.

Cinemation comes with a program called CinePlayer, which you can distribute with your presentations so other people can play them on their Macs.

Vividus offers a cool selection of clip animations (see figure 4.24) as an optional add-on to Cinemation (or any other animation program for that matter). The animations are provided as scrapbook files—you can use them with any program that supports cut and paste.

Figure 4.24

Cinemation clip
animation

Animation Works

Gold Disk Inc.
3350 Scott Boulevard, Building 14
Santa Clara, CA 95054
Phone: (408) 982-0200 or (800) 835-5889
Fax: (408) 982-0298

List price: $199

System requirements: 2M RAM for color, 1M for black-and-white (in addition to system requirements), System 6.0.5 or higher.

Animation Works is comprehensive cel animation program specifically designed for creating cool animations. Like most of the others, it features a character editing window (see figure 4.25) that allows for onion-skinning sequential frames of a character. It also has path-based animation tools for defining a character's path across the screen.

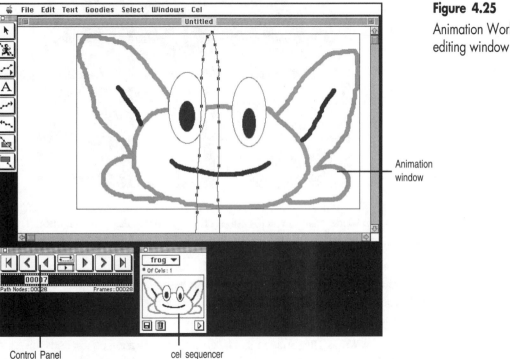

Figure 4.25

Animation Works's character editing window

Where Animation Works really excels is in all the little details it adds for creating smooth, convincing animations. One of the coolest of these is the *hierarchical motion* feature. This takes the form of a Magnet tool, but its uses are endless for an animator (see figure 4.26). For example, if an airplane drops a bomb, the bomb doesn't fall straight to the ground; it accelerates toward the ground, but continues moving forward at roughly the speed of the airplane. This results in a motion path that arcs smoothly forward to the ground. In Animation Works, you can make any motion path the parent of another motion path. In another example (as in figure 4.26) the Moon can turn around the earth while the Earth revolves around the Sun.

51

Figure 4.26

Animation Works's example using the hierarchical motion feature

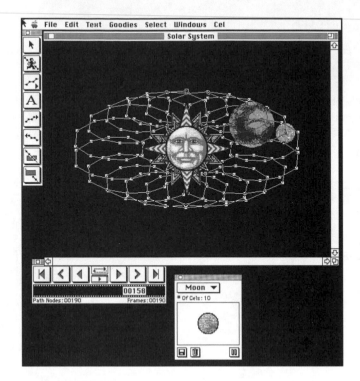

Animation Works enables you to easily set the Ease-in and Ease-out of motion. This controls an object's acceleration and deceleration so that it doesn't simply jump into action.

The program's painting tools are pretty unusual, too (see figure 4.27). It has a good selection of primitive shapes, such as arcs. It also enables you to create brushes that conform to shapes and paint with patterns. You can also fill a shape with a gradient that conforms to the shape's contours. On the other hand, Animation Works supports only 256 colors.

Animation Works's Registration tool is very intuitive. Clicking on a cel sets the registration point at the spot where you clicked, but if you hold the Command key and click, it sets the registration point and jumps to the next cel.

In contrast to the other cel animation programs that stress interactivity, Animation Works offers only a Loop Event command, that causes an animation to cycle through a segment of animation until you click the mouse.

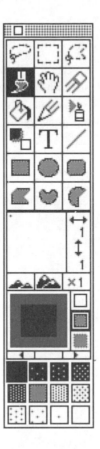

Figure 4.27
Animation Works's painting tools

The program includes a Movie Player that you can distribute with your animations so people can play them, and it includes a HyperCard XCMD for playback of animations in HyperCard.

Another nice feature of Animation Works is that it comes with a video tape tutorial that quickly teaches you the program's basics.

Summary

Cel editing software enables you to create traditional style frame-by-frame animations. Advantages over traditional methods are many. You can easily reorder and play back frames, and onion-skinning makes it easy to create smoothly flowing characters. You can overlay unlimited layers and animate characters using paths—thus overcoming the serious limitations of hand-drawing on acetate.

The next chapter, "Warping and Morphing," takes animation a step beyond cel animation, to digital special effects. Instead of creating the illusion of motion by joining subsequent cels, this software allows you to move the individual pixels of a single image or cel.

Warping and Morphing

Digital processing has made strange and wonderful advances in animation. Though digital animation is sometimes known as special effects, this book concentrates on the two main types of digital processing known as *warping* and *morphing*. Unlike cel animation, these techniques rely on manipulation of existing images. They take existing pixels—from illustrations or photos—and push, pull, and transform them over time. The user defines the beginning and ending states, and the software does all the thinking. Unlike a paper photograph that would be torn to shreds by this kind of handling, digital effects software maintains the continuity between areas in an image, even as it distorts them beyond all reasonable grotesqueness.

Warping

Warping is relatively easy to comprehend, at least as far as the basic definition goes — among other things, it means stretching, squashing, twisting, and distorting. When you warp an image, you are stretching regions of it into strange shapes (see figure 5.1). The trick to warping software is that it has to accomplish this stretching without visibly enlarging the pixels in distorted areas, which would result in unwanted digital artifacts.

Figure 5.1

The amazing
warping dog

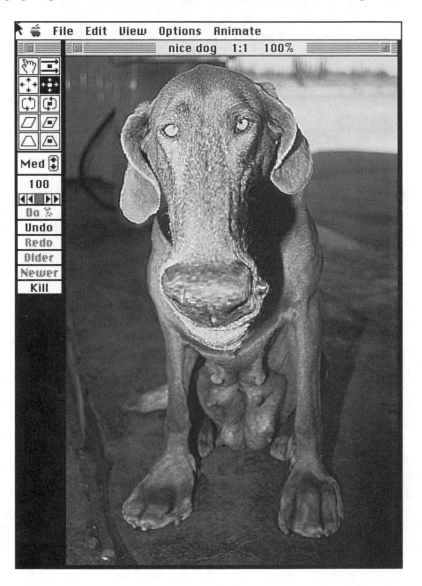

To date, Flo', its big brother, Metaflo', Elastic Reality, and Morph 2.0 are the programs with a warped sensibility. Flo', the demo software included with this book, is the only program devoted exclusively to warping.

Morphing

The word morph is short for metamorphosis, and that word implies changing shape. Morphing, as far as Mac users are concerned, implies changing one image into another over time. You've seen Michael Jackson do this in music videos and morphing has sprouted up in lots of other places as well.

Essentially, morphing works by blending together various regions of two different pictures until the first picture becomes the second (see figure 5.2).

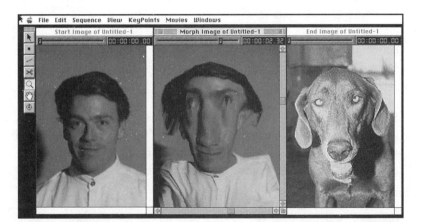

Figure 5.2
Morphing melds two images.

Convincing morphs seamlessly blend images into one another, without viewers being aware that they're actually seeing a sophisticated dissolve between two pictures.

One program is currently dedicated to morphing for the Mac: Gryphon Software's Morph version 1.1, the program that introduced the genre to Mac users. A high-end QuickTime special effects program, Video Fusion, also offers morphing as one of its many special effects. In addition, Motion Works's Utilities includes a program called Mini Morph, with many of the same capabilities.

Warped-morphs and Other Monsters

While they're actually very different effects, warping and morphing go together like Dracula and Frankenstein. Fortunately, for twisted individuals who need to do both — separately or at the same time — no less than three programs combine these two effects: Gryphon Software's Morph 2.0 (available concurrently with version 1.1), ASDG's Elastic Reality, and the VALIS Group's Metaflo'. The beauty and horror of this duo of features is that objects can warp into new shapes before they morph... ad nauseam.

Flo'

The VALIS Group
P.O. Box 422
1001 West Cutting Boulevard
Point Richmond, CA 94807-0422
Phone: (510) 236-4124
Fax: (510) 236-0388

List price: $199

System requirements: Flo' requires a fairly souped-up Mac for the simple reason that warping a digital photograph requires tons of complex processing. You'll need a Mac II or later with System 7, 8-bit color or better and QuickTime installed. You'll also need 8M of RAM and a math coprocessor (FPU). If you don't have an FPU in your Mac, you can get by with a freeware program called FPU, available from many online services. This tricks your Mac into thinking it has an FPU, but it won't provide the critical function of an FPU which is speeding up intensive floating point math calculations required for digital image processing. In other words, use FPU and your Flo' will be slow. (See chapter 9, "Downloading Software" for information about how to get a copy of FPU.)

Disk: The hot new demo version is included on the *Cool Animation Disk*.

Flo' is the epitome of coolness. It brings new meaning to the word "twisted."

Not only can Flo' be used to create freaky and supernatural transformations of perfectly normal-looking pictures, but it's also possible to create really subtle and disturbing animations — make George Washington break a smile from the face of the one dollar bill, watch Richard Nixon's nose grow long, or make Abraham Lincoln wiggle his ears.

How Flo' Works

As we described in chapter 1, Flo' works on the principle of a photograph applied to a flexible rubber sheet.

Flo' offers the following tools for both Local and Global transformations: Translation, Scale, Rotate, Skew, and 4-point distortion. Global tools affect the entire image. You can use them for creating interesting perspective effects, or to make a picture look like it's falling over, for example. In general, they're more subtle and not as bizarre as things you can do with the Local tools.

The Local tools allow you to transform only selected areas of an image. For example, you can select just a person's eyebrows and forehead. Once you've selected this region, warping tools allow you to move, scale, push, twist, or stretch it in an unlimited number of ways.

Flo' maintains the smooth relationship of warped and unwarped parts of an image so they appear to be perfectly "natural" extensions of each other.

The variety of transformations you can achieve in this manner will forever warp your sense of creativity.

Your First "Flo'mation"

1. Assuming you followed the directions for unstuffing your *Cool Animation Disk* onto your hard drive and installing QuickTime, all you need to do is double-click the Flo' Demo icon in the "Cool Mac Animation" folder. This will open up the Flo' workspace.

2. After Flo' opens, choose **Place...** from the **File** menu. Select the image named "Dude" in the "Cool Images" folder and click on Open (see figure 5.3).

3. Make this the first key frame of your animation by selecting **Start Key** from the **Animate** menu.

4. Select the Global Distort tool from the tools palette, click on the image, and drag the corners together until they almost touch (see figure 5.4). Click on the image.

Figure 5.3 Global tools   Local tools

The Dude

Move —
Scale —
Rotate —
Skew —
Distort —

controls
smoothness of —
the distortion

controls
percentage of
a distortion to
render

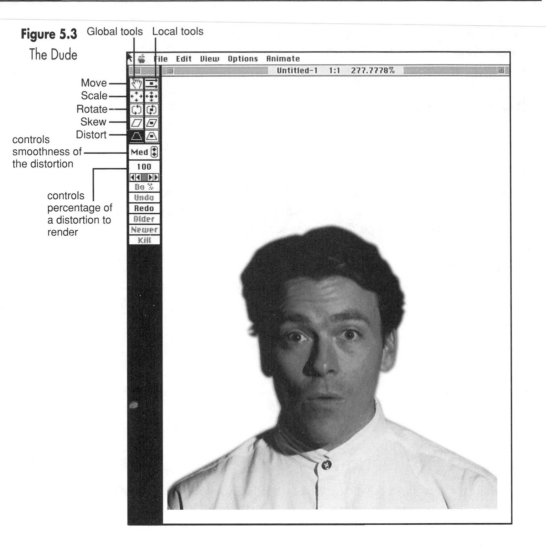

5. After Flo' completes the transformation, choose the **Add Key...** command in the
    Animate menu and set the number of in-between frames to 10 (see figure 5.5). Click
    on OK.

Figure 5.4

Using the Global Distort tool to start the transformation

6. Choose the `Create QuickTime Movie...` command from the `Animate` menu, set the compressor to Animation (see figure 5.6). Click on OK. After entering the filename for your animation, you can set size and resolution. For now, accept the choices in the dialog box.

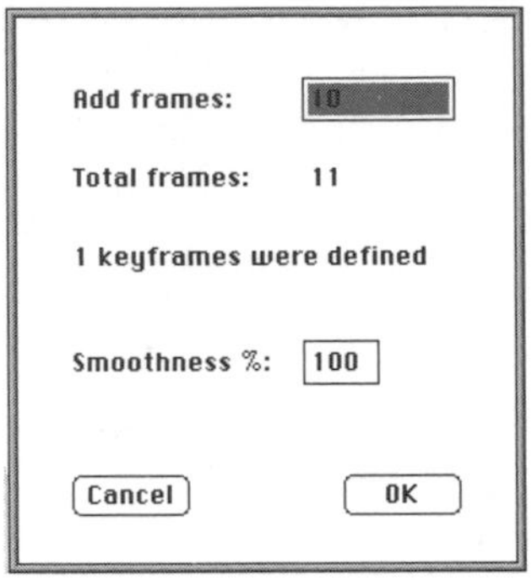

Figure 5.5

Setting the number of in-between frames

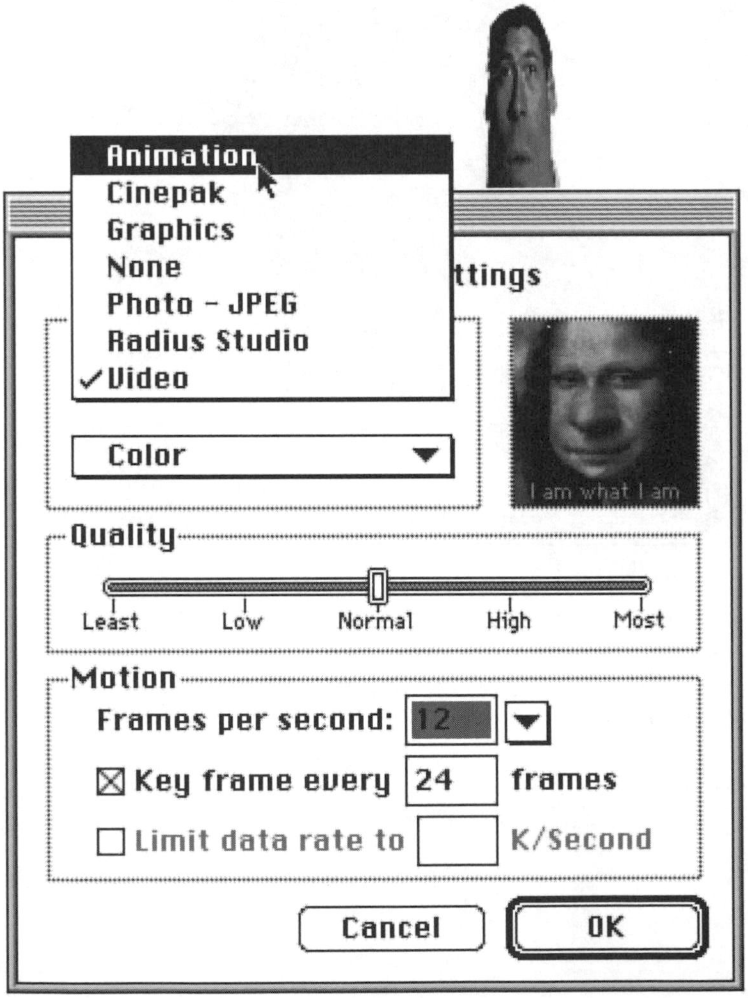

Add frames:	10
Total frames:	11
1 keyframes were defined	
Smoothness %:	100

Cancel   OK

Figure 5.6

Setting the QuickTime compressor to Animation

Animation
Cinepak
Graphics
None
Photo – JPEG
Radius Studio
✓Video

...ttings

Color ▼

I am what I am

Quality
Least   Low   Normal   High   Most

Motion
Frames per second: 12 ▼
☒ **Key frame every** 24 **frames**
☐ **Limit data rate to** ___ **K/Second**

Cancel   OK

7. Wait for Flo' to generate the animation. When it's done, open the movie with the Apple Movie Player to view it (see figure 5.7).

Figure 5.7
Viewing the animation

Local Warping with Flo'

The most basic kind of Local warp involves a simple stretch, squash, or rotation of a selected area. One great feature of Flo' is that it offers unlimited Undos, and you can even Undo intermediate steps without undoing subsequent ones. This gives you unlimited room to experiment with your animations. It also offers a good way to step backwards and forwards through parts of your project prior to generating an animation.

1. Once you're comfortable with Global transformations, it's time to create a new project and jump into Flo's super-cool Local distortions. If your global projects are open, close them and make a new file.

2. Select **Place...** from the **File** menu and choose the file "Dude" again.

3. Now for the fun part: Using the Local Scale Selection tool from the Flo' palette, draw a perimeter around the upper half of the subject's head as shown in figure 5.8.

4. Using the Scale tool, grab the selection and drag the mouse toward the top of the Boundary and release. Flo' calculates the transformation (see figure 5.9).

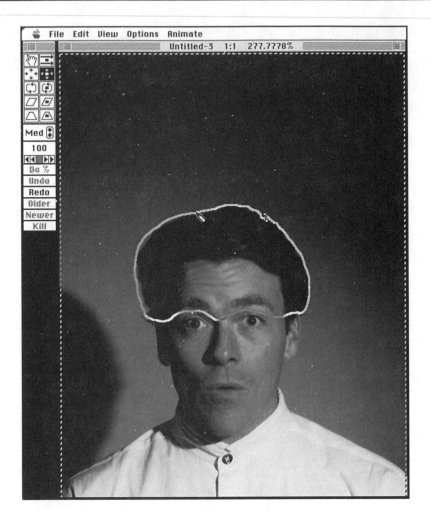

Figure 5.8

Designating the area
to transform

Tip:
Although you're distorting a selected area, keep in mind that just as with a rubber sheet that you gather in the middle, the effects of a distortion usually affect the image all the way to the edges; to protect parts of the image, you have to "pin them down" by creating a Boundary selection.

5. To set the size and other parameters of the movie you'll create, choose **Render Size...** from the **Options** menu. As shown in figure 5.10, leave the resolution at 72 dpi, and set the size to 240 by 320 pixels. (You have to deselect the "Maintain current render aspect ratio" option to do this.)

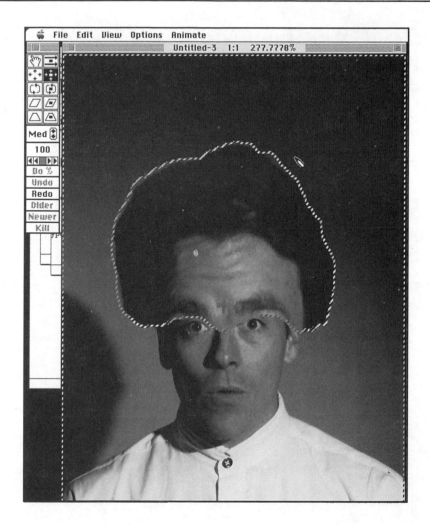

Figure 5.9
Stretching a head

6. Go to the first frame of the sequence using the Undo button and choose the **Start Key** option in the **Animate** menu. Now go to the last frame of the project using the Redo button and choose **Add Key...** from the **Animate** menu. Enter 10 for the number of in-between frames to add (see figure 5.11). Click on OK. You now have two *key frames*, the start frame and the end frame. Each key frame defines a critical point in the animation. Save the project using the **Save...** command in the **File** menu (use a name other than "Dude").

7. Choose **Create QuickTime Movie...** in the **Animation** menu, choose the Animation Compression, and specify the filename Dude's Head and press Save. Then sit back and wait for Flo' to generate the animation (see figure 5.12).

Figure 5.10

Determining size and resolution

```
┌──────────────────────────────────────────────────────────────┐
│             ▤▤▤▤▤  Rendered Size and Resolution  ▤▤▤▤▤          │
│  ┌─────────────┐                                               │
│  │ Render=Work │    Work         Render      % Render/Work     │
│  └─────────────┘                                               │
│                                                                │
│  DPI horiz.        200        ┌────────┐    ┌────────┐         │
│                               │  72    │    │  36    │         │
│  DPI vertical      200        │  72    │    │  36    │         │
│                               └────────┘    └────────┘         │
│                                                                │
│  Inch width        2.655      ┌────────┐    ┌──────────┐       │
│                               │ 3.3333 │    │ 125.549  │       │
│  Inch height       3.415      │ 4.4444 │    │ 130.144  │       │
│                               └────────┘    └──────────┘       │
│                                                                │
│  Pixel width       531        ┌────────┐    ┌──────────┐       │
│                               │ 240    │    │ 45.1977  │       │
│  Pixel height      683        │ 320    │    │ 46.8521  │       │
│                               └────────┘    └──────────┘       │
│                                                                │
│  Render kilobytes: 225                      ┌────┐  ┌────────┐ │
│  ☒ Maintain current render aspect ratio     │ OK │  │ Cancel │ │
│                                             └────┘  └────────┘ │
└──────────────────────────────────────────────────────────────┘
```

Figure 5.11

Setting the number of in-between frames

```
┌──────────────────────────────────────┐
│                                        │
│   Add frames:      ▌10▐                │
│                                        │
│   Total frames:     11                 │
│                                        │
│   1 keyframes were defined             │
│                                        │
│                                        │
│   Smoothness %:    │100│               │
│                                        │
│                                        │
│   ┌──────────┐       ┌──────────┐      │
│   │ Cancel   │       │   OK     │      │
│   └──────────┘       └──────────┘      │
│                                        │
└────────────────────────────────────────┘
```

8. When the movie's done, double-click on the animation to launch the Movie Player and view your freaky new creation. (If you're short on RAM, you may have to quit from Flo' to launch the Movie Player.)

Getting Tricky

Flo' can do a lot more than make your head swell. There are several tricks to creating more complex animations. The first is to use the Boundary and Core tools to isolate areas being transformed; the next is to use multiple transformations on separate parts of the image; finally, you can separate some of these transformations with key frames so that transformations happen in multiple stages.

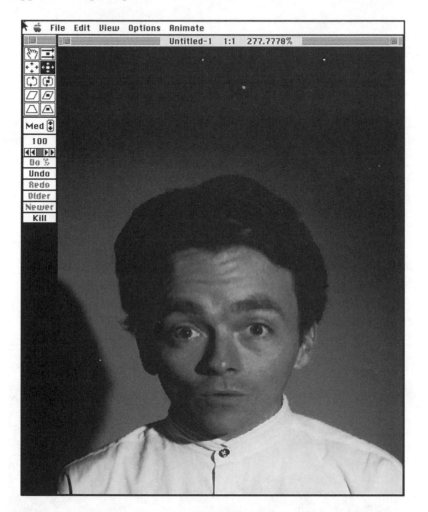

Figure 5.12
The Dude's Head (a major pain in the neck)

You've already discovered how to create a Core selection; you simply draw a region using a Local transformation tool. This defines the region to be transformed. A Boundary, in contrast, defines the limits of the region you're transforming, thereby protecting parts of the image you don't want distorted. For example, you may want to enlarge a nose without affecting the entire face. To do this, select the nose as a Core, then hold down the Command key and draw a selection surrounding the nose (with enough margin between them to accommodate the nose's growth).

You can apply many of these transformations to a single image, growing here, shrinking there, rotating this, and distorting that. The result is sure to look very different than the original, although you'll be surprised how recognizable it is.

At any point in this process, you can set a key frame and define a number of tween frames, so that each transformation may take place simultaneously, in rapid succession, or can be strung out one-at-a-time.

The following example shows all of these techniques combined where the last example left off.

1. Flo's **View** menu allows you to set a magnification to zoom into an image for detail work. The Hand tool in the toolbox allows you to pan the image around in the workspace without affecting your work. Using these features, zoom into the Dude's mouth. Select **Start Key** from the **Animate** menu.

2. Using the Local Scale tool, draw a Core selection just around the perimeter of the lips.

3. Holding the Command key, draw a Boundary around the Core selection, this time extending it to encompass the facial muscles surrounding the lips (see figure 5.13).

Figure 5.13

Selecting the Dude's mouth

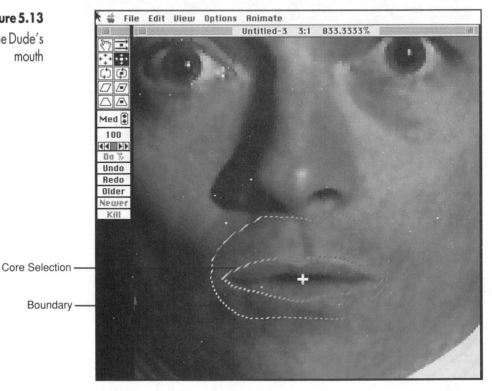

Core Selection ———

Boundary ———

4. Still using the Local Scale tool, drag the Core to shrink it to a small area in the middle of the Boundary (see figure 5.14). Wait for the warp to complete and notice that the Boundary acts as a perimeter for the warp — it protects the region outside from being changed. Meanwhile, the Core selection defines the area to change and the extent of the change (see figure 5.15).

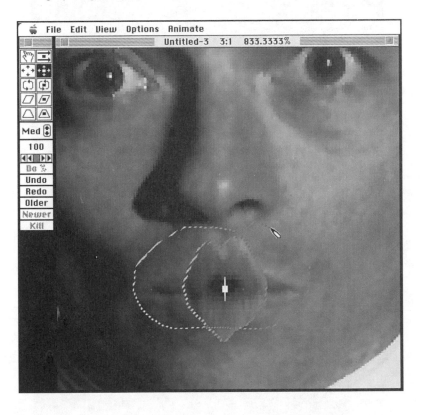

Figure 5.14
Shrinking the Core

5. Now select the Dude's chin with the Local Translate tool (see figure 5.16). Create a narrow Boundary (Command-drag) that surrounds the chin selection and extends down near the bottom of the image and drag the selection towards the bottom of the image (see figure 5.17). Once this transformation is complete (see figure 5.18), use the **Add Key...** command and set 10 tween frames.

69

Figure 5.15

Puckering up

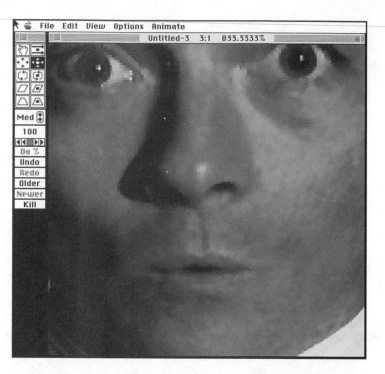

Figure 5.16

Selecting the Dude's chin

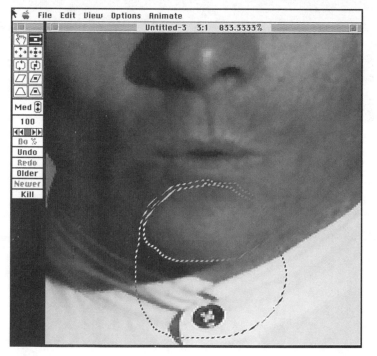

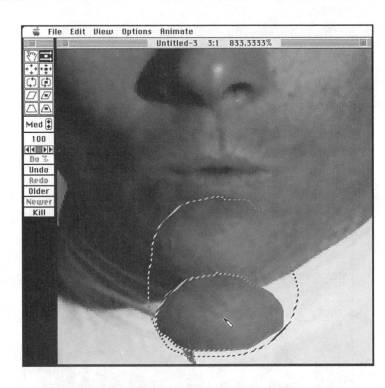

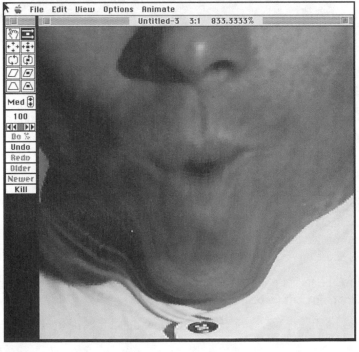

Figure 5.17
Extending the chin

Figure 5.18
By the hairs of his chinny chin chin

71

6. The next change is made to the Dude's right eye. In this case, the Local Scale tool is used to define a Core surrounding just the eye and eyebrow and a Boundary is set to allow room for their enlargement without distorting the rest of the face (see figure 5.19). Note that the Boundary is very near the Core at the bottom. That's because you don't want the cheek to be deformed by the transformation.

Figure 5.19

Defining Core and Boundary

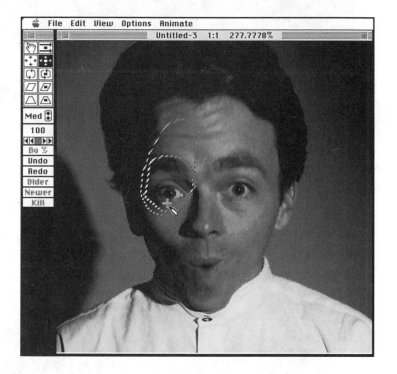

7. Since you're enlarging the eye upward only, move the transformation point down near the bottom of the selection (see figure 5.20). This will cause the enlargement to originate from this point, meaning the nearly the whole Core will enlarge upward. (Imagine using a push pin to anchor the rubber sheet at this point.)

8. Drag on the core to enlarge it upward. Figure 5.21 shows the finished(?) eye.

9. The final transformation is to rotate the head. In this case, we use the Local Rotate tool to select the head as the Core. By not defining a Boundary, Flo' defaults to using the entire image as the limit of the transformation (see figure 5.22).

10. Move the anchor point to the area near the neck; in this case, it will be used as the pivot point for the rotation.

11. Drag on the Core selection to rotate it approximately 20 degrees (see figure 5.23).

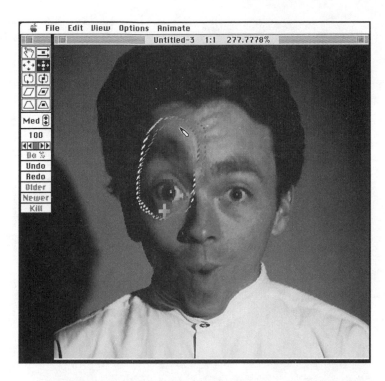

Figure 5.20
Enlarging the eye upward

Figure 5.21
Highbrow Dude

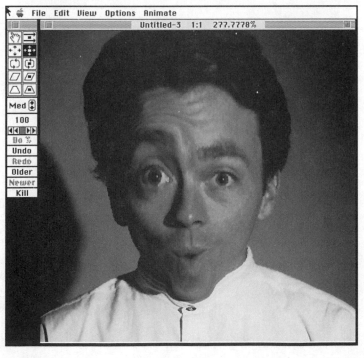

Figure 5.22
Selecting the head as the
Core

Figure 5.23
Rotating the head

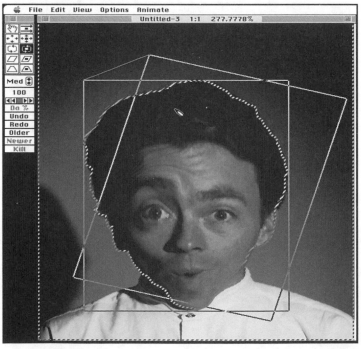

12. Use the **Add Key...** command and insert 10 tween frames. Follow the procedures from the previous example for generating a QuickTime movie. Figure 5.24 shows the final Dude.

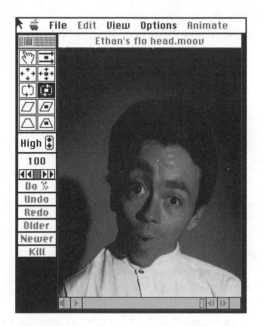

Figure 5.24
The Final Dude

Final Notes on Flo'

Flo' has many other tools to enhance your warped creations. You can render quality settings, alter the smoothness of transitions between one frame and the next, and you can work with alpha channels. (If you generate a warp of an image that uses an alpha channel, the alpha channel is warped as well, meaning you can seamlessly composite the animation.)

While the demo version of Flo' limits you to a particular set of images, the commercial version has no such restrictions. It's equally as good for creating images for print as it is for creating animations for multimedia and video output.

Metaflo'

Metaflo' is the VALIS Group's professional version of Flo'. Like Flo', it allows you to generate warped and twisted images from digital pictures. The most significant difference is that it also allows you to morph from one image to another while you warp them. This means you can generate an animation of your mother swelling into a balloon which suddenly becomes your father. Ugh!

Metaflo', in our humble opinion, is the only special-purpose special effects animation program for the Mac that's cooler than Flo' itself.

Morph 2.0

Gryphon Software Corp.
7220 Trade Street, Suite 120
San Diego, CA 92121
Phone: (619) 536-8815
Fax: (619) 536-8932

List price: $239

System requirements: System 7 or higher, color monitor, 5M RAM (in addition to system software), 10M hard disk space. (8M of RAM and a 40M hard disk recommended.)

The program that launched the whole Mac FX Animation craze was a low-cost utility called Morph. *Morphing*, as we've already explained, is short for *metamorphosis*, as in caterpillars turning into butterflies, and Morph takes this role seriously. (But not so seriously that it isn't fun.) Morph also offers warping tools in the latest version.

How Morph Works

In Morph, you begin by importing two thematically similar images. The most common example is to bring in two faces. (They needn't be similar faces. In fact, they don't have to be similar species.) You then establish regions of similarity by clicking on the start image with a Point tool, then dragging corresponding points on the end image into corresponding positions. For example, you can define the left eye of the start image by clicking on the two corners and the top center and bottom center edges; corresponding points will appear in the same location on the end image. You then drag these to the corners and top and bottom edges of the end image's left eye. Once you have defined both images completely in this way (see figure 5.25), you are ready to generate a morph.

You can preview the progress of your morph by dragging a slider in the Morph window, or you can simply generate a QuickTime movie, specifying the image size, frame rate, and QuickTime compressor.

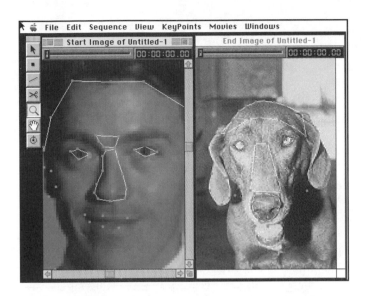

Figure 5.25
Corresponding points
designated in two images

Moving Morphs

Morph can also be used to morph together two segments of moving video. This requires some careful planning and direction while filming the original video segments, otherwise it's very difficult to get moving frames to match each other. For example, in the start movie, the left eye of the actor is visible, while in the end movie it's not.

Even when creating morphs from static images, it's worthwhile to prepare the images so that they have common characteristics. The most important example of this is the background; morphs will appear much more convincing if the backgrounds are the same for both images.

While Morph works by blending the contents of target regions together, it's possible to fine tune the blending levels so you don't see both the starting and ending images blurred together, which can ruin the morph effect. This pops up frequently when you're trying to morph very detailed contrasty images such as two line drawings.

Morph is capable of morphing only points or only colors as well as doing both (see figure 5.26).

Caricatures

Morph 2.0 has a special feature for creating caricatures. You've seen caricatures in many cartoons—political cartoons, in particular.

Figure 5.26

Morph's Custom Crossfade
dialog box

Custom Crossfade...

Points	Colors
○ Crossfade	◉ Crossfade
◉ Start Only	○ Start Only
○ End Only	○ End Only
○ Past End	

[Cancel]   [OK]

Tip:

A caricature is an image that exaggerates distinctive features of a person. Richard Nixon's ski-jump nose, Jimmy Carter's horse teeth, and Ronald Reagan's pompadour are common examples. While these features weren't all that impressive in real life, they became permanently associated with those former presidents.

Morph's approach to caricature isn't as pithy as Gary Trudeau's, but it's still pretty cool.

To create a caricature, the start image should be that of a "plain" person. The end image is that of your subject. When you generate a caricature, Morph compares "ordinary" features of the Start image to the "unusual" features of the end image. It then begins with the end image and extrapolates an animation far beyond it that blows the differences out of proportion. It takes some experimentation, but the results can be hilarious.

Warping

Morph 2.0 also does warping, basically by filling the shape of the end image with the colors of the start image (or vice versa). While it's often a convincing effect, it's not nearly as—eh, hem—fluid as Flo's.

Morph 1.1

Morph 1.1 is almost unchanged from the original version. As this book was going to press, it was still possible to buy the older version, so we included it here. It has the same basic interface as Morph 2.0 for creating basic morphs. The key difference is that it's only set up for doing one Morph at a time (Morph 2.0 will string them together); it can't handle morphs of moving images; and it doesn't do warping. If you're just after simple morphing, it's still the least expensive option and it's a lot of fun.

MiniMorph

Motion Works Inc.
524 Second Street
San Francisco, CA 94107
Phone: (415) 541-9333 or (800) 800-8476
Fax: (415) 541-0555

List price: $249 (bundled with the Motion Works Utilities)

System requirements: Not available at press time.

MiniMorph is a morphing program intended to be very similar in scope to Gryphon's Morph version 1.1. It wasn't shipping in time to be included in this book, but the company planned to give it basic morphing capabilities without warping.

Elastic Reality

ASDG Software Inc.
925 Stewart Street
Madison, WI 53713
Phone: (608) 273-6585 or (608) 271-1988

List price: $349

System requirements: FPU and color, 8-bit, 8M RAM, System 7.01, QT 1.5 or later, hard disk.

Elastic Reality is ASDG's port of its powerful SGI workstation morphing software. While it's designed to do the same thing as Morph, it has a number of features which make it more flexible, more complicated to learn to use, and ultimately more powerful. Like Morph, Elastic Reality begins by having you import a starting and ending image. However, you can actually import a whole series of images if you like; they are all added to ER's A/B Roll window which resembles those in QuickTime editing programs (see figure 5.27).

Once you've imported your images, you define morphing regions by drawing regions with a Bezier pen tool which resembles the tools used by Aldus FreeHand or Adobe Illustrator (see figure 5.28).

After a number of shapes are defined, you can combine them into groups, which makes it easier to copy, paste, and move them around (see figure 5.29).

Figure 5.27

Elastic Reality sequencer

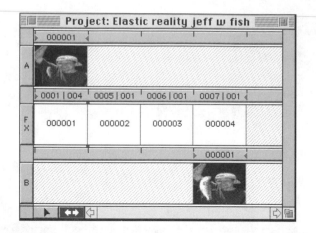

Figure 5.28

Original image

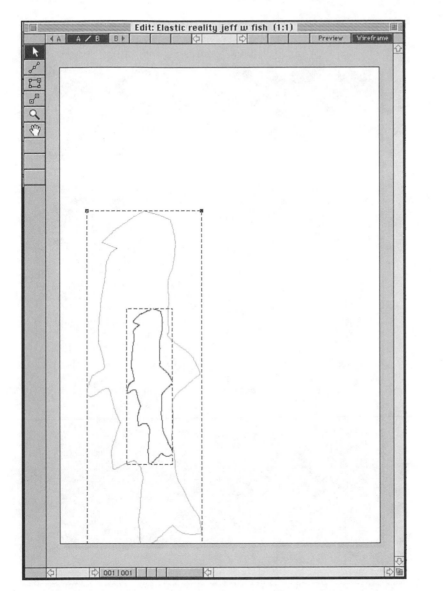

Figure 5.29
Blueprint for a growing fish

Figure 5.30 shows you a preview of Elastic Reality's handiwork. Unfortunately, it won't help your local taxidermist.

Figure 5.30

Fish stories are all the same.

Elastic reality is the only morphing package that allows you to specify different rates of dissolve and motion for different parts of an image. This means you can have the eyes morph suddenly, while the rest of the face morphs over a long time.

The program also has extensive features for controlling fine points like ease-in and ease-out of effects (see figure 5.31).

Figure 5.31
Elastic Reality options

Summary

Warping and morphing are the oozing edge of Mac animation. Warping is the bending, twisting, stretching, and squashing of images as if they're printed on Silly Putty. Morphing takes one image and, seemingly by magic, transforms it into another.

In the next chapter, "The Third Dimension," you'll learn how to to make realistic 3-D animations, the ultimate form of which is 3-D objects that morph into one another!

The Third Dimension

3-D software works by offering you a virtual 3-D world. Objects you create have not only height and width, but also depth. When you animate a 3-D object, it can fly freely in virtual space. It can soar around unconstrained by the laws of physics, but this object can also have the properties of real objects, including color and texture, and it can be subject to the influences of light and shadow. It's possible to create animations of airplanes flying down supermarket aisles and submarines lurking in the depths lava lamps because an object can be animated in front of photographic backgrounds and even other animations.

What you see happening as objects fly around is based on your point of view. This is similar to looking at a television screen and seeing a scene as viewed by a remote television camera. The cool catch is you get to play director! The camera can be placed anywhere you like inside the scene. You can zoom it in extremely close to see tiny details on an object's surface, or you can pull way back, as if you were viewing the scene from the Goodyear Blimp.

85

There are two Mac 3-D software programs that currently qualify for *Cool Mac Animation* awards: Pixar's Typestry and Specular International Inc.'s LogoMotion. There are lots of other 3-D animation programs available, with prices starting abound $800, but Typestry and LogoMotion are each available for under $200.

3-D animation involves four separate phases:

1. Modeling, which is the building of objects you intend to animate

2. Scene building, which is the placement of models, lights, and textures

3. Animation, which is the moving around of objects

4. Rendering, which is the process the computer uses to calculate what all of these details would look like if they were real objects floating around in real space

Modeling

There are many possible ways to model an object in 3-D. LogoMotion and Typestry both rely primarily on a process called *extrusion*. You can think of extrusion as cookie cutter modeling. You begin with a 2-D shape (probably the most common example is font outlines). When you extrude these letters, you specify the depth of the "cookie dough" and the type outlines are used as cookie cutters. What you end up with are perfectly cut out 3-D objects, as shown in figure 6.1.

Figure 6.1

3-D extruded type

3-D programs offer one enhancement over cookie cutters when extruding: you can add subtle or extreme *bevels* to the edges of objects. Look at any manufactured object (a wooden table is a typical example) and you'll notice that the edges aren't perfectly sharp corners. They have subtle curves to them. These bevels not only make objects less dangerous, they also make them look nicer. Bevels can be applied in many different styles, and if you look at a whole bunch of different manufactured objects, you're likely to see several types. Figure 6.2 shows an example of beveled type.

Figure 6.2
3-D beveled type

Both LogoMotion and Typestry specialize in using fonts as starting points for modeling. However, it's also possible to import outline shapes from a drawing program like Adobe Illustrator to use as starting points. A really cool way to utilize fonts as fodder for cool 3-D objects is to begin with a symbol font, such as Zapf Dingbats or Letraset's Fontek Naturals fonts. Symbol fonts are made up of small pieces of artwork that have been saved in the form of a font, with a different drawing assigned to each letter on the keyboard (both upper and lower case).

Scene Building

Once you build a model, you can add texture to its surface. This can be as simple as a color and level of glossiness, or as complex as multicolored dragon skin or mahogany wood grain.

Typestry and LogoMotion have very different approaches to this process, so each is covered separately where we discuss the specific products.

Another crucial part of scene building is lighting. Just like a photographer needs to light his models before he takes a picture— either with sun, flash, flood lights or spotlights—the 3-D artist has to place lights in the scene to illuminate the models.

Both Typestry and LogoMotion have special tools that let you place lights and move them around in a scene.

Finally, you have to be able to position all of your models so that they're in proper alignment in the scene. This is just like getting everybody together for a big family photograph. The obvious question you're going to ask is, "I can understand how to drag a model up and down and left and right on the screen, but how do I move it in and out along the third dimension?"

The answer is pretty simple. You position all of your objects looking at the scene from the front, then you switch your point of view (typically with a menu command) to look down on the scene from the top. Now, as you move the objects around, you're moving them in-and-out as well as left-and-right. When you're done, you can switch back to a front view to see your changes.

Incidentally, you can also change your point of view to see the scene from the side.

One final element of scene building is setting your *focal length*. If you've ever used a camera with a zoom lens, you'll understand immediately what focal length does. Simply, you can zoom in and out from your scene to see more detail, or to fit more stuff into view. Figure 6.3 demonstrates what some 3-D type would look like if photographed with a normal lens.

Figure 6.3

Normal lens

Like a real camera, using a very wide-angle lens results in a distorted image (you've probably seen wide-angle pictures of people photographed very close up, with their gigantic nose filling up the image and their tiny head seeming very far away.) Figure 6.4 demonstrates the effect a wide-angle lens would have on figure 6.3's type.

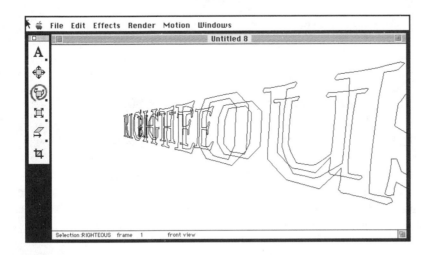

Figure 6.4
Wide-angle lens

Animation

3-D animation is really no different than scene building, except that to create an animation, you use something called key frames. The way animation works is that you build a scene, set a key frame, then move around the objects in the scene. You can also alter the lighting, change the camera's focal length, and make any other changes you want to happen. When you're finished making changes, set another key frame. When you generate an animation, the software remembers the state of your virtual world at the first key frame then tweens all of the changes evenly until it reaches the second key frame. For instance, you could create a logo, drag it off the screen, and set the first key frame, then drag the logo to the center of the screen and set the second key frame. When you generate an animation, the logo will automatically fly onto the screen and stop at the center of the scene. Because changes can take place in three dimensions, you can make objects fly around each other, or dance and bounce around the scene.

You can also set more than two key frames. The beauty of using the Mac, as usual, is that it does all of the difficult drudge work of calculating the in-betweens.

Rendering

Once you set up an animation, you can render it. Rendering is the process the computer uses to take all of the information you've provided—models, textures, lights, and action—and then generate a realistic-looking 3-D animation.

This is probably the most distinctive part of every 3-D program. LogoMotion and Typestry have very different rendering schemes. What they have in common, however, is that rendering is pretty slow, no matter what you do. It takes millions of calculations to simulate the play of light on solid surfaces, and like all animation, the Mac has to do it for many frames.

While there are many distinct types of rendering available to Mac animators, Typestry relies on a unique form of rendering called RenderMan, while LogoMotion uses a shading technique called Gouraud. Neither of these methods is as realistic as the most impressive rendering method available, *ray tracing*. This method accurately depicts shadows, mirror reflections, and the refraction of light as it passes through transparent surfaces. However, ray tracing is extremely slow (so it requires a top-of-the-line Mac), and it's difficult to implement in software (so it's expensive). To date, the only under-$500 Mac 3-D ray tracer is Ray Dream's Designer, but it doesn't do animation.

LogoMotion

Specular International Inc.
479 West Street
Amherst, MA 01002
Phone: (413) 253-3100
Fax: (413) 253-0540

List price: $149

System requirements: Mac II or better, 5M free RAM.

One of the newest and coolest animation programs to come along for the Mac is Specular's LogoMotion. This program is like the kid sister of Specular's high-end 3-D program, Infini-D. (A working demo version of Infini-D is available on Hayden's online forum. See chapter 9, "Downloading Software.")

LogoMotion is a full-fledged 3-D program that allows *lathing*, as well as extrusion. While extrusion works like a cookie cutter, lathing spins an outline around an axis. You can visualize how lathing works by bending a piece of coat-hanger wire into a crooked shape,

then spinning it very rapidly by gripping one end between your flattened palms and rubbing them together; the resulting blurry image is similar to what you'll get when you lathe the wire's outline.

There are several ways to create shapes in LogoMotion. Initially, you choose an extrude object, a lathe object, or type from the tool palette and click in the drawing window. In the case of an extrude or lathe object, this places a simple geometric shape in the window, while in the case of type, a dialog box asks you to enter a *type string* (commonly known as a *word*) and specify a font to extrude.

Extruding Type

To extrude type, select the Type tool in the main tool palette and click on the work window. In the type dialog box, enter a type string and select a font. LogoMotion asks you to specify an *extrusion depth* and bevel. Revisiting the cookie-cutter metaphor, extrusion depth is simply the thickness of the cookie dough.

Once you've made all your selections and click OK, a wireframe model of your extruded type will appear in the LogoMotion Camera window. This is a solid object which can now be given a texture, stretched, squashed, enlarged, reduced, rotated around any axis, and animated (see figure 6.5).

Figure 6.5
Wireframe model showing extrusion depth

To rotate the object, for example, you simply choose one of the rotation tools from the tool palette, select the object in the Camera window and drag the mouse around. Note that there are separate rotation tools for each of the 3-D axis—x,y and z (see figures 6.6, 6.7, and 6.8).

Figure 6.6

The extruded type

Move (horizontal and vertical)

Move (horizontal and in-out)

X-axis Rotate
Y-axis Rotate
Z-axis Rotate
Uniform Scale
Squash and Stretch
Type Object
Extrude Object
Lathe Object

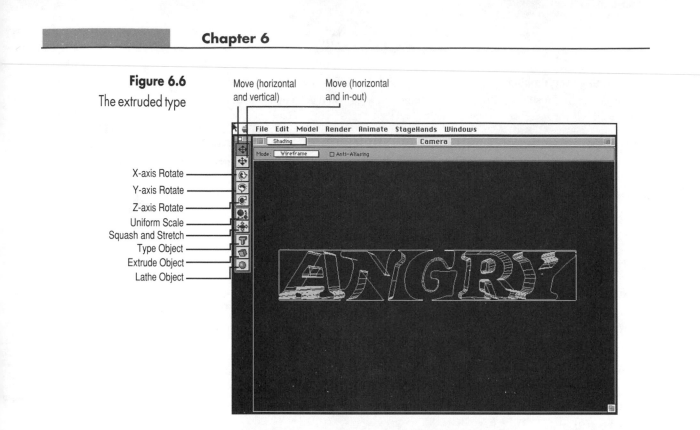

Figure 6.7

To rotate the object around the x axis, select the X-axis Rotate tool, then click on the object and drag it downward.

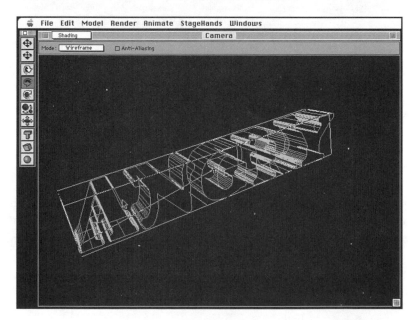

Figure 6.8
Result of rotation

Extrusion Objects

As with type, LogoMotion can extrude 2-D outline artwork. This includes illustrations created in drawing programs like Adobe Illustrator and Deneba's Canvas. You can also extrude encapsulated PostScript (EPS) artwork from clip-art disks.

To create an extrusion, choose the Extrude tool and click on the Camera window to place an extrude primitive. This is a generic shape whose outline you modify to create a specific extruded object. Double-click on this object to open the Extrusion Workshop. You can either modify the outline by clicking and dragging on points or you can replace it altogether by importing artwork from another program.

LogoMotion supports System 7's Publish and Subscribe, so you can modify your outlines in another program, such as Illustrator, and have the changes automatically reflected in your 3-D objects.

Once you've finished modifying your 2-D outline, choose an extrusion depth and bevel, just as with the Type dialog box. The result is a 3-D version of your 2-D artwork.

Extruding a Shape

1. Select the Extrude tool and click on the workspace window to place an extrude primitive (a cube is shown in figure 6.9).

Figure 6.9

Placing a generic extrusion object in the workspace window

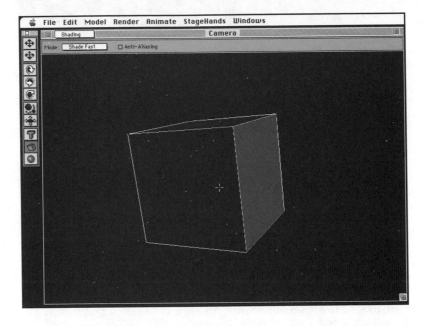

2. Double-click on the model to open the Extrude Workshop (see figure 6.10).

Figure 6.10

Opening the Extrude Workshop

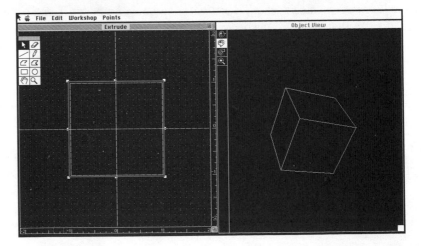

3. Select the Polygon drawing tool from the tool palette and draw a new shape in the left-hand window (see figure 6.11).

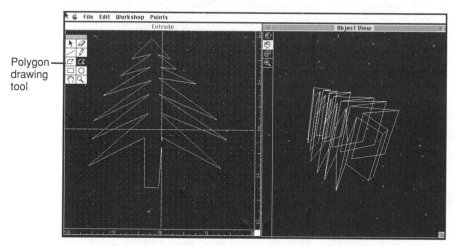

Polygon drawing tool

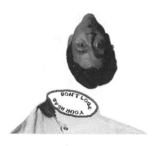

Figure 6.11

Use the Polygon drawing tool to create a new shape.

4. Choose the **Bevel** command from the menu and select a bevel from the pull-down menu. You can modify this curve by dragging around the vertex and you can choose whether or not to apply a bevel to the back face of the object (see figure 6.12). When you're satisfied, click OK.

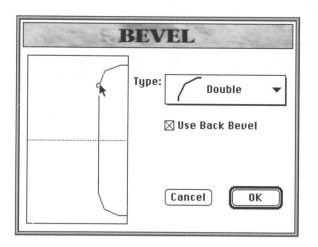

Figure 6.12

Modifying the bevel

5. In the work window, choose **Shade Best** from the pull-down menu at the top of the window to see a rendered version of your creation (see figure 6.13).

Figure 6.13

Viewing the final
rendered image

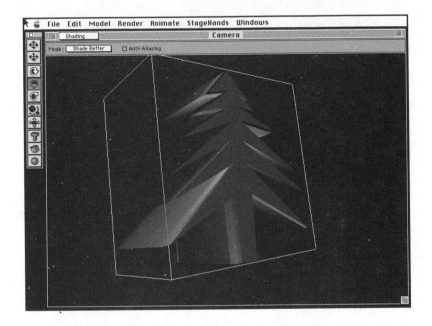

Lathing a Rocket

Lathing in LogoMotion is very much like extrusion, except that in the Lathe Workshop the 2-D outline you supply is revolved around a straight axis in the perspective window. The result is an object with the outline you supplied and a round cross section along its axis. The following sequence shows a simple shape being lathed into a round rocket form.

1. Select the Lathe tool and click on the workspace window to place a generic lathe object (see figure 6.14).

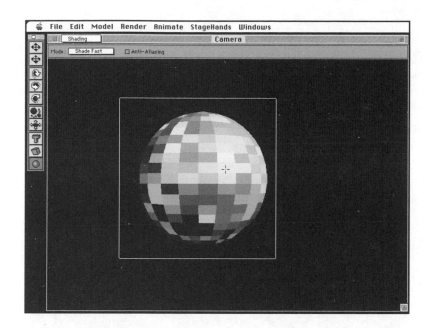

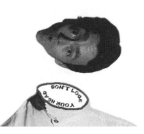

Figure 6.14
Placing a generic lathe object
in the workspace window

2. Double-click on the model to open the Lathe Workshop.

3. Select the Reshape Outline tool from the points menu palette and modify the outline by dragging points of the line around in the 2-D view (see figure 6.15). You can create a new outline from scratch by selecting one of the drawing tools and simply drawing in this window.

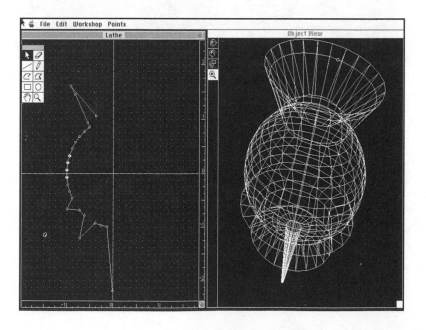

Figure 6.15
Modifying the object's outline

Tip:

As with the Extrude Workshop, you could also use the Subscribe command to work interactively with a program that supports Publish and Subscribe, such as Illustrator or FreeHand, or you could subscribe to an outline created previously; when you update the outline and Publish it, the model will be automatically updated in LogoMotion.

4. If you want a bevel on the corners of your lathed shape, you create it by putting a bevel into your outline (see figure 6.16). When you're satisfied, click OK.

Figure 6.16

Beveling the corners of the shape

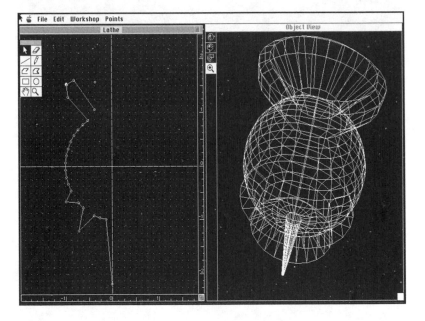

5. In the work window, choose **Shade Best** from the pull-down menu at the top of the window and wait to see a rendered version of your creation (see figure 6.17).

98

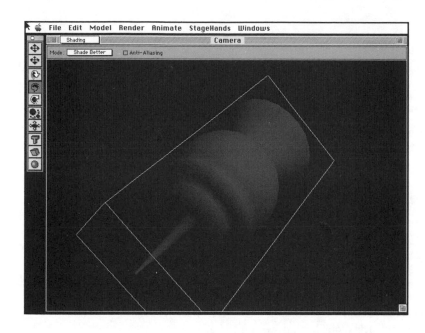

Figure 6.17
Viewing the final rendered image

Setting the Scene

Once you've created the objects you want to animate in LogoMotion, it's time to give them surface qualities (such as metallicity, color, and reflectivity), adjust their sizes, and move them into position. To give an object a surface quality, select a texture from the New Texture pop-up in the Object menu. LogoMotion does this with a simple set of sliders for metallicity, color, and reflectivity (see figure 6.18).

Figure 6.18
Setting surface qualities

To adjust an object's size, use the Uniform Scale tool. By simply dragging on the object, it shrinks or grows, depending on the direction of your mouse's movement. The Stretch tool is used to adjust the size of an object along one axis at a time.

Positioning an object is a little more complicated. The easiest way to see what you're doing is to open one or two windows in addition to the Camera view. You do this through the `Views` pop-up. For example, once you've opened the Top and Right views, it's possible to see your scene from several angles at once. Any change you make in one view is automatically updated in the others. For instance, if you move left an object in the Front view, it will also move left in the Top view. You won't necessarily see the change in the Right view, however.

Lights

LogoMotion features a wide variety of StageHands, which are extensions to the program that automatically handle activities like setting lights, placing props and backgrounds, and setting environments (which give reflective objects their shine). Using StageHands, it's easy to place Hollywood-style spotlights and overhead flood lights.

You can set the color of lights in a scene, which allows you to adjust their brightness as well. (For example, to dim a white light, make it gray.)

Environments

Another important feature of a 3-D scene builder is the capability to change a model's *environment*. An environment consists of two elements: the background or scenery against which you place your models (this is often a scanned image or a hand-drawn picture) and the *reflection environment*. In LogoMotion there are no true ray traced reflections since the rendering method is Gouraud, but surfaces still reflect their environment. This is important for making a reflective or metallic surface look real; without reflections, every object you create would look like dull plastic. You can choose from a variety of reflection environments in LogoMotion.

Tip:
Take a look at a shiny object, such as a piece of chrome, a brass doorknob, or a polished spoon. Notice that there are many blurry reflections of the surroundings on the surface of the object. These surroundings are the object's environment.

Animating 3-D Objects

LogoMotion offers an animation system that's just like the one in Infini-D. This is a sophisticated *event-based sequencer*. The sequencer has a row for every object in your scene with time along the top. Every time you make a change to an object, such as moving, rotating, or changing its color, the change is recorded at the current time on the object's time line in the sequencer. Change the current time by dragging a marker to a new position on the top row. You can make an unlimited number of changes along the time line. Each of these changes, called an *event*, is indicated by an event marker.

When you choose the `Make Movie` command, LogoMotion will automatically tween all of an object's changes from one event to the next. Preview the tweened animation by clicking the Preview button. This generates an animation using only bounding boxes to represent the 3-D objects, but it gives you a good idea of how your animation is working out.

Creating a Simple Animation

The easiest way to create animation in LogoMotion is to extrude an object, then animate it along a simple motion path.

1. Select the Type tool and click on the Camera window.

2. Enter a text string, select a bevel, set the extrusion depth to 0.300 and click OK (see figure 6.19).

Figure 6.19
LogoMotion's Text dialog box

3. Assign a Gold texture to the object in the `Render/Apply Surface...` menu.

4. The Sequencer window (see figure 6.20, bottom) is where you control the key events of your animation. Make sure the time marker is all the way to the left, at time 00.00. Place the logo in its starting position using the Move and Rotate tools.

Figure 6.20

Setting the sequencer and positioning the logo

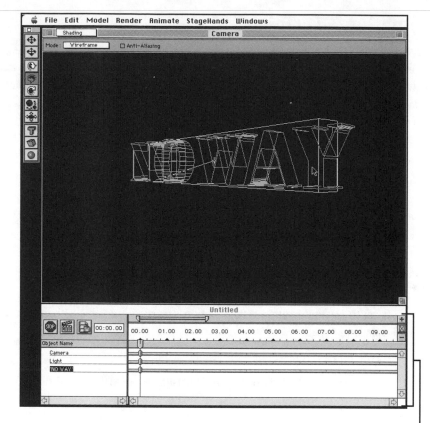

Sequencer window

5. Drag the time marker in the sequencer to 03.00 (three seconds) and move the logo to its ending position (see figure 6.21).

6. Click on the Preview button in the sequencer to preview a wireframe of the animation.

7. Choose `Make Movie...` from the `Animate` menu and set the rendering quality level (see figure 6.22).

102

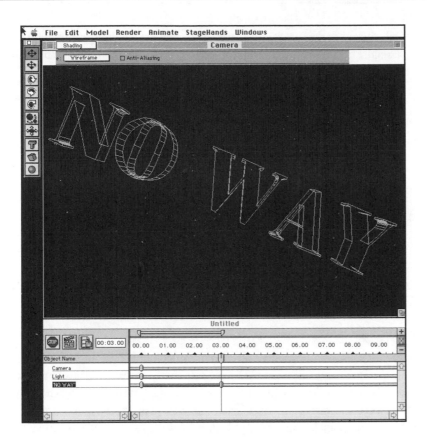

File Edit Model Render Animate StageHands Windows

Shading   Camera
Wireframe   ☐ Anti-Aliasing

Untitled

STOP   00:03.00   00.00 01.00 02.00 03.00 04.00 05.00 06.00 07.00 08.00 09.00

Object Name
Camera
Light
NO WAY

Figure 6.21
Repositioning the logo at
03.00 seconds

MAKE MOVIE

─Render "Untitled"──
Quality: Shade Better ▼   Options...

Width: 320   Height: 232
☒ Constrain Proportions

Colors: Millions ▼
☒ Create Alpha Channel

Frames: ◉ All   ○ From: [___] ▼   To: [___] ▼
Rate: 15 ▼ Frames/Second

Cancel   Render...

Figure 6.22
Setting the animation and
rendering parameters

103

8. While the movie renders, it is displayed in the Camera window, one frame at a time (see figure 6.23). Once the movie is complete, you can open and edit it with the Movie Player.

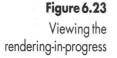

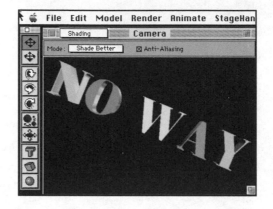

3-D Morphing

LogoMotion can do 3-D morphing—an extremely cool and sophisticated form of 3-D animation that smoothly changes one 3-D object into another over time. The way you do this is to specify "snapshots" for a single object at points on the time line. After each snapshot, open the object in a workshop and edit its characteristics. Taking a snapshot freezes the state of the object at that point in time, and LogoMotion knows to tween between the two frozen states of the object.

Creating a Flying Logo Morph

1. Launch LogoMotion. In the **StageHands** menu, choose **Backdrop** and select the CloudScape picture (see figure 6.24).

104

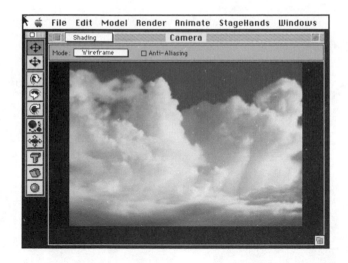

Figure 6.24
Choose a backdrop.

2. Select the Type tool and click on the Camera window. When the dialog box opens, type your first name with an apostrophe-s (´s) (see figure 6.25). Enter a depth of 0.300, select a simple bevel and a font, then click OK.

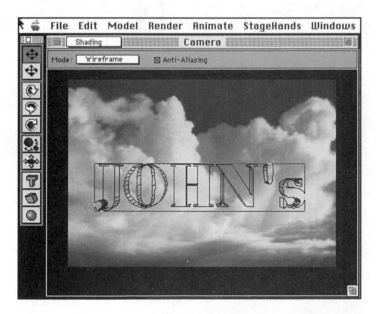

Figure 6.25
Place text onto the backdrop.

3. Move this logo so that it's centered in the camera window.

4. Choose `Gold` from the `Render/Apply Surface...` menu (see figure 6.26).

Figure 6.26

Add a gold texture to the text.

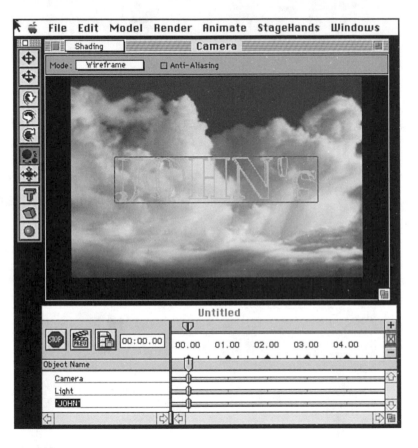

5. Using the animation sequencer, drag the time marker to 1 second (01.00). Choose `Snapshot` from the `Animate` menu (see figure 6.27).

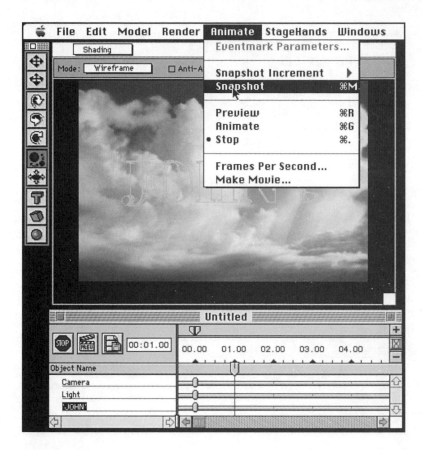

Figure 6.27
Choose Snapshot from the Animate menu.

6. Drag the time marker to 2 seconds (02.00). Double-click on your name logo. The type dialog box will open up. In the space where your name is, type the phrase way too and click OK. You now have a 3-D logo that says "way too" where your name used to be (see figure 6.28).

Figure 6.28

Replacement 3-D type

Note:

When creating a shape morph in LogoMotion, it works best if the objects being morphed have the same number of parts—adjust your text strings accordingly.

7. In the **Render/Apply Surface** menu choose a chrome texture.

8. Choose **Snapshot** again to freeze this frame.

9. Move the time slider to 3 seconds (03.00). Double-click on the "way too" logo. Enter cool!! and click OK (see figure 6.29).

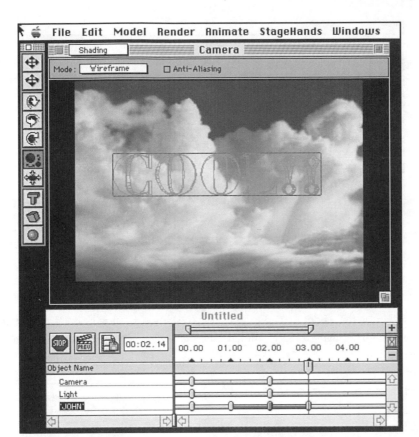

Figure 6.29
Another replacement
logo

10. Give "cool!!" a green texture.

11. Select the **Snapshot** option.

12. Click the Preview button in the Sequencer. LogoMotion will show your animation from beginning to end, representing objects with bounding boxes.

13. The final stage is to add some motion to the camera, so it's clear to viewers that we're working in cool 3-D. Open a Top View window and zoom it out so you can see the camera as well as your 3-D objects. Move the time slider to 00:00 and move the camera to the right and rotate it to the left so it's still aimed at your logo. Note how the view changes in the Camera window (see figure 6.30).

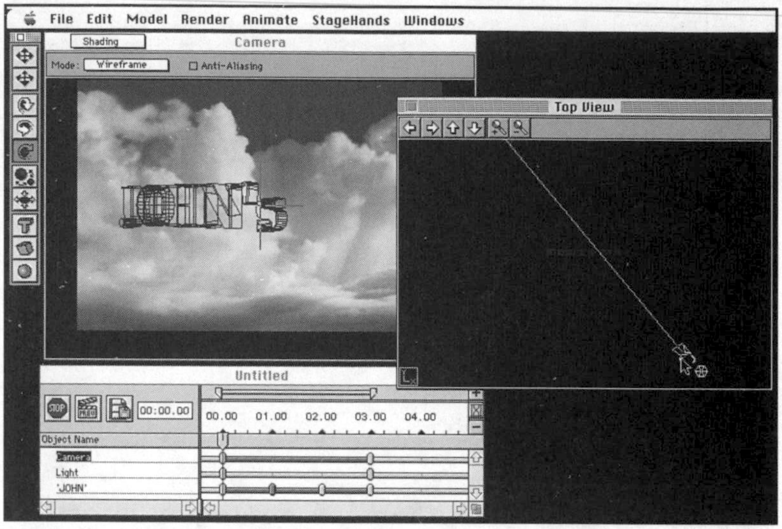

Figure 6.30

Viewing your logo from a new angle. The camera is rotated in the Top View window in the foreground.

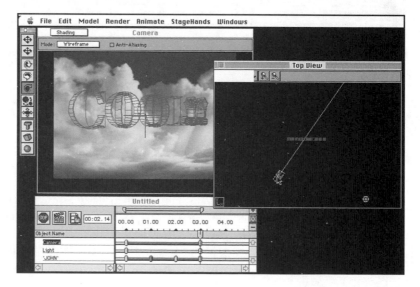

14. Move the time slider to 03:00. Reposition the camera by moving it left and rotate it slightly to the right so it stays pointed at the logo. Again, note the change in the Camera window (see figure 6.31).

Figure 6.31

Viewing your logo from a new angle at 03:00 seconds.

15. The final step is to generate the QuickTime animation. Choose `Make Movie...` from the `Animate` menu, set the shading options to Shade Better, the frame size to 320 by 240, the range of frames to All and the frame rate to 15 fps (see figure 6.32). Click the Options button and set the animation options to Animation/millions/better.

Figure 6.32

The Make Movie...
dialog box

16. Wait for LogoMotion to render the final movie (see figure 6.33).

(a)
Figure 6.33

Four frames of the final movie

111

(b)

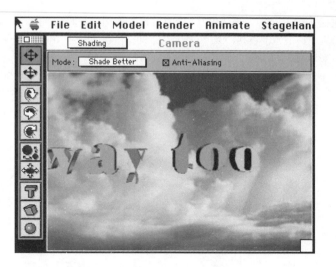

(c)

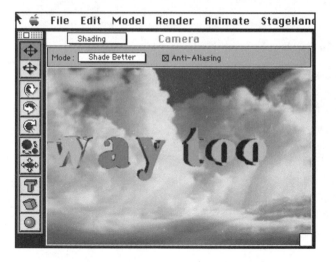

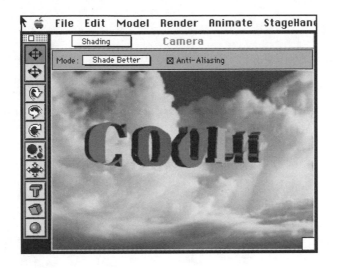

(d)

Typestry

Pixar
1001 West Cutting Boulevard
Richmond, CA 94804
Phone: (510) 236-0388
Fax: (510) 236-0388

List price: $299

System requirements: color Mac, with 8M RAM (12M recommended), 8M hard disk space, System 7 or later.

Pixar's Typestry was the first low-cost 3-D animation program for the Mac. When it first came out its animation capabilities were a little tame, but as this book was going to print, Pixar was putting the final touches on a low-cost 3-D animation monster that included such futuristic effects as particle emission, which allows you to create sparkling 3-D objects and other cool stuff.

Like LogoMotion, Typestry helps you create 3-D models from typefaces. It also enables you to import and extrude 2-D artwork created in Adobe Illustrator (or any other program that can save Illustrator-format files). Typestry lacks the capability to lathe objects. (Pixar's high-end program, ShowPlace, has lathing and extrusion bells and whistles as well as many others, but no animation.)

Extruding Type

You extrude type by selecting the Type tool and clicking in the working window. A dialog box prompts you to enter a type string (see figure 6.34). Once you've entered the characters to extrude, you can choose a bevel from a huge set of preconfigured curves, or you can define your own using the built-in bevel editor (see figure 6.35). Setting the extrusion depth is simply a matter of dragging a slider. Once you click OK, your extruded object becomes a 3-D wireframe model in the work window (see figure 6.36).

Figure 6.34

Enter a type string.

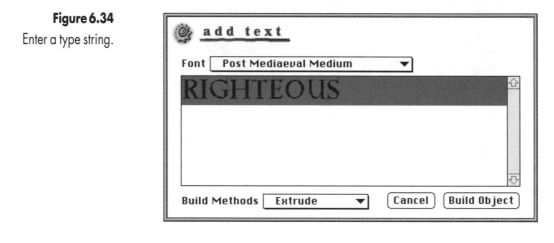

Figure 6.35

Choose a bevel.

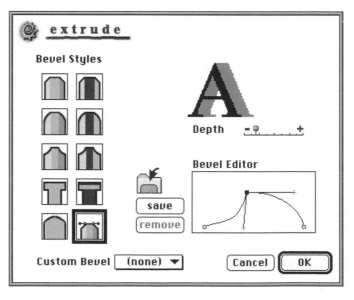

Figure 6.36
Display a 3-D
wireframe model.

One really useful feature of the new Typestry is that you can group and ungroup objects. For example, you can group all the surfaces of a character together. If you apply a texture to any part of the group, *every* part will be surfaced with the texture. On the other hand, if you ungroup the character, you can apply different textures to the sides and faces. You can also name groups and select objects and groups by name, which is important when you have lots of wireframe models on the screen and you can't tell which one you're clicking on.

Extruding Illustrator Art

Importing Illustrator or FreeHand artwork is by far the most useful way to get art into a 3-D program for most graphic artists. These two programs (and Deneba's Canvas) are the most popular ones for creating 2-D line art. They make it very easy to draw complex, cool 2-D logos and such. Since Typestry can import illustrations created in these programs, now it's easy to draw a starting shape and turn it into a realistic 3-D model. Of course, anything you model in this way instantly becomes available for animating.

Building a Scene

Building a scene in Typestry is extremely easy. Essentially all you do is drag models around on the screen, and occasionally change your point of view to look at the scene from a different angle.

Typestry creates very realistic textured surfaces, complete with shadows, bumps, and simulated reflections.

Looks

Typestry comes with a library of textures, known as Looks (see figure 6.37). One of the coolest things about Looks, is that they are *procedural shaders*. That is, they create a texture based on a wide range of mathematical procedures, rather than use a predefined image. Using a built-in feature called Glimpse (a separate program with ShowPlace) you can change the parameters of these procedures to create all kinds of modified versions of Looks textures. For instance, a Look called Dragon Skin (created by the VALIS Group, creator of Flo') can be modified to look like strange variegated orange skin or even rolling, multi-colored foothills, in addition to alligator hide.

Figure 6.37

Some of the many Looks to choose from

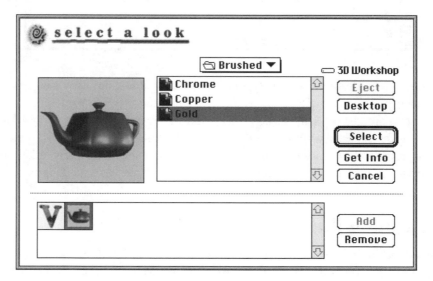

Because of their very rich textures, Typestry's renderings are generally much more lifelike than those created in LogoMotion. One good example of this is bumps. Bumpy, lumpy, crackled, gnarly skin may not seem like a glamorous thing to you, but consider the fact that the vast majority of 3-D programs are unable to create bumps on skin. They can only create bumpy shadows and highlights; the edges of a skin remains perfectly smooth. In Typestry, bumpy skin actually has *displacement*, that is, the bumps look and act like real bumps.

Imagine an orange with perfectly smooth skin, or a gravel driveway, or a logo encrusted with gemstones. These surfaces just don't look real without real bumps, which is why I can say Typestry is one of the best programs available for creating realistic renderings.

Lighting

Typestry's lighting is simplistic when compared to LogoMotion's. Typestry uses a lighting panel which shows lights on a pair of grids mounted in front of and behind the scene (see figure 6.38). You can switch on or off any of the lights on these grids. You can also adjust the intensity and color of the light sources, as well as the *gel* used for each light. A gel in the real world is a colored piece of glass or plastic through which you shine a light. This can also include silhouette shapes such as window blinds or eves, which will cast shadows onto your model for creating a mood.

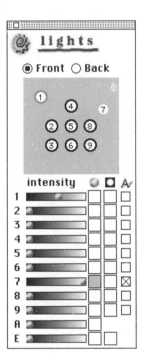

Figure 6.38

Typestry's lighting panel

The lighting palette also lets you specify an environment (for simulating reflections on an object's surface) and ambient light (which has no direction and is used to soften harsh shadows).

Another type of lighting is provided in the form of shaders. These are similar to Typestry's textures (in fact, they rely on the same procedural process), but applying them results in lighting up a scene. It's a little confusing, but procedural lighting's really cool once you get used to it.

Setting a Scene

To set a scene in Typestry, you begin by creating a model. In this example, you'll use a clip art font. (A clip art font is a font made up of artwork posing as type characters.)

1. Choose the Type tool and click on the work screen.

2. Enter a character from the font by typing a "letter." Enter a depth by dragging the slider and select a bevel (see figure 6.39).

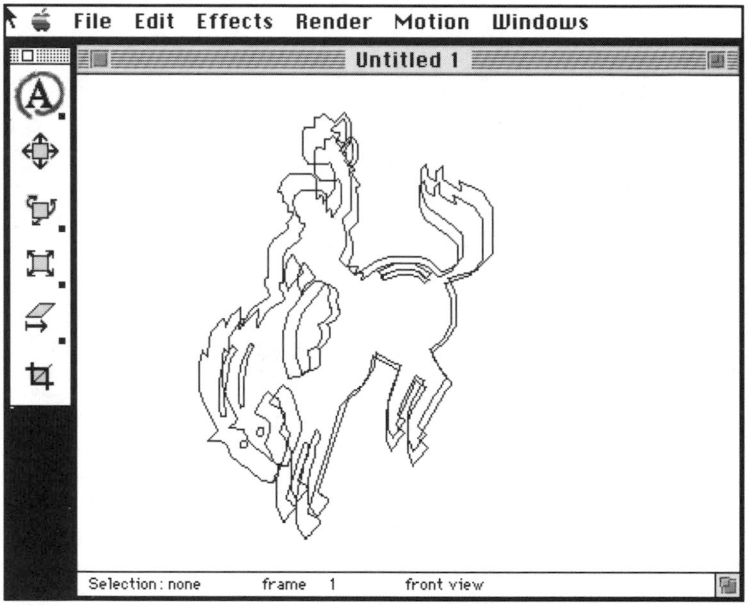

Figure 6.39

Add depth and a bevel to a character.

3. Move the logo into position with the Move tool, and use the Rotate tool to slightly spin around the logo and give it a good sense of perspective (see figure 6.40).

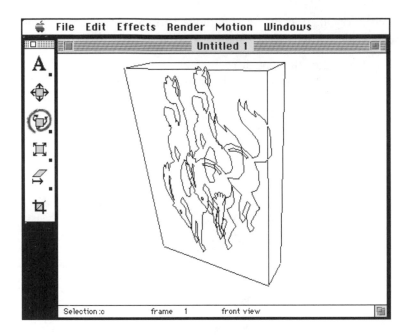

Figure 6.40
Adjust the camera's perspective

9. With the logo still selected, open the Looks window and choose a texture from the palette. Note that you can apply different textures to sides and faces (see figure 6.41).

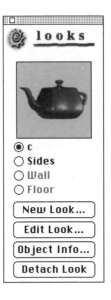

Figure 6.41
Apply a "Look" texture

119

10. Open the Lighting palette and click on the light in the upper-right corner (number 7). Set this light to white and full intensity (see figure 6.42).

11. Click on the light in the upper-left corner (number 1) and set the color to deep blue and the intensity to about two-thirds of maximum.

Figure 6.42

Set two lights.

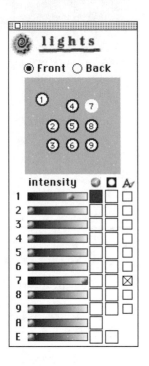

12. In the **Effects/Backgrounds...** menu, check **Wall** to place a wall behind the logo.

13. Use the **Render/Render** to screen menu to select the **Preview quality** setting.

14. Wait for the rendering to finish (see figure 6.43).

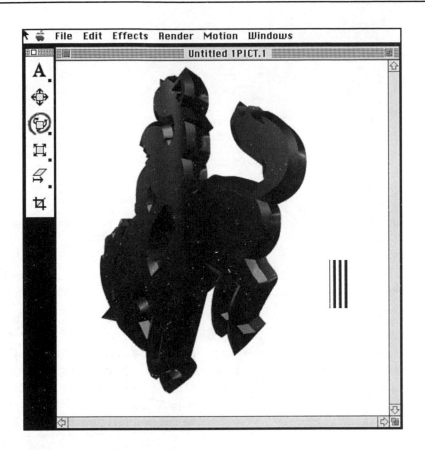

Figure 6.43
View the finished
scene.

Animation Features

Animating objects in Typestry is extremely similar to animating objects in LogoMotion. Once you create a model and position it on the screen, you can position a time marker in the animation sequencer and move, rotate, scale, or otherwise change the model to set an event (see figure 6.44). Because Typestry automatically breaks a type logo into a grouped hierarchy, it's easy to select one letter of a logo, or another part of a group, and animate it independently of the parent object.

121

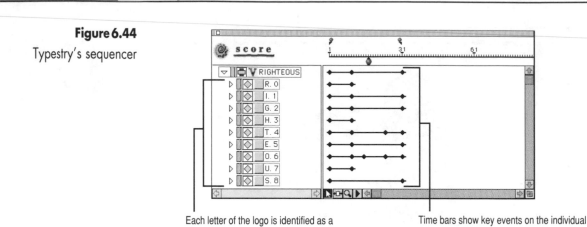

Figure 6.44

Typestry's sequencer

Each letter of the logo is identified as a separately animatable character.

Time bars show key events on the individual timelines of each character.

The real power of this approach comes from the fact that animations themselves are hierarchical. If you move a parent, the child objects move with it; on the other hand, you can move a child object without affecting the parent.

Particle animation on high-end systems lets you blow things up or turn them into bits which can be rearranged into other objects. Typestry is the first program anywhere near the Cool Mac price range to offer particle animation. (Previously, the least expensive particle animator was StrataStudio Pro, at $1,495.) On the other hand, it's not full-blown particle animation—you can't blow things apart—it's more like a light show. You can have a 3-D model, such as a logo, emit a shower of sparks or bubbles. It's a cool effect not found anywhere else on the Mac.

Rendering

Where Typestry really excels is in rendering. The program relies on RenderMan, which is the same rendering technology offered by Pixar's high-end 3-D program, ShowPlace. It's also the same underlying rendering technology used by Industrial Light and Magic, and other wizards of Hollywood special effects. (Although Hollywood wizards are worlds removed by virtue of in-house programmers, massive computer networks, and gigantic animation budgets.)

RenderMan offers many advantages over other kinds of rendering, most particularly, it's platform independent. This means you can take a scene created on one computer, and render it on any other computer running RenderMan, including Windows machines, NuBus accelerator boards, and giant networks of high-speed UNIX computers.

On the other hand, without a super computer to do your rendering, RenderMan can be one of the slowest renderers out there. If you're the kind of person who likes to see things finished, and make lots of little changes, RenderMan can be brutally slow (keep in mind that animations require many separate renderings).

Summary

Three-dimensional animation enables you to create ultra-realistic models of real-world objects which you can animate in 3-D space. This allows for all kinds of creations never before possible on a Mac (or anywhere else, for that matter).

3-D animation is best broken down into four basic stages (even the Apollo moon rockets went in stages): modeling, scene building, animation, and rendering. Modeling is the creation of models; scene building is the positioning of the models, the application of textures, and lights; animation involves moving and changing models at individual key points in time; and rendering is where the Mac generates the final realistic animations.

As with all Mac animation programs, LogoMotion and Typestry (and the other Mac 3-D programs) are especially suited to creation of QuickTime files. To edit these files and add special effects, sounds, and transitions, you'll want to learn about QuickTime editors and effects programs, covered in the next chapter.

QuickTime Effects

While almost every program created with Mac animation in mind now supports QuickTime, a new class of software is specifically designed for editing and adding special effects to QuickTime. After all, it's one thing to be able to save an animation, it's another to be able to smoothly edit together animation segments and to add transitions and sound tracks.

QuickTime editors are an invaluable part of any Mac animator's toolbox. While it's possible to get by with the very simple animation tools, such as Apple's Movie Player, the more sophisticated your animations become, the more you'll want a program that provides advanced editing and effects.

125

Some of the low-cost programs discussed here are the scaled-down baby siblings of high-end QuickTime editors such as AVID's VideoShop and Video Fusion's Video Fusion. If and when you decide to move into the world of professional animation, familiarity with QuickFlix or Sparrow will make it very easy to move up to the professional versions.

One of the best reasons to use a commercial QuickTime editor, rather than just using the Movie Player, is that programs like QuickFlix and Sparrow support alpha channel and color key compositing. This means you can easily layer together many segments of animation.

Another important consideration is that these programs give you high-level control over QuickTime settings, such as video compressors, frame rates, and sound compression.

If you're lucky enough to have access to video digitizing hardware, QuickTime editors allow you to capture video from a VCR or video camera and turn it into raw material for creations that straddle the line between animation and video. Even if you can't digitize video, you can use QuickTime editors to create elaborate, professional-looking movies with lots of special effects, transitions, and multi-layer sound tracks, using material you create from scratch with animation software that saves QuickTime movies.

Movie Player

Apple Computer, Inc.
20525 Mariani Avenue, MS 336
Cupertino, CA 95014
Phone: (800) 282-2732

Price: Free on the *Cool Animation Disk*!

System requirements: Movie Player only requires about 400K of free RAM, but the more RAM you have, the better your movies will play back.

Apple's Movie Player is the simplest of all QuickTime editors, but you'd be surprised how much you can do with it. Best of all, you get it for free on the *Cool Animation Disk*!

The Movie Player has a simple VCR-style interface (see figure 7.1). When you open a movie, you can play it by pushing the Play button and fast forward and rewind it with corresponding buttons. The most interesting part of the Movie Player comes from using the slider bar in conjunction with the Mac Clipboard. By holding Shift and dragging the slider, you can select any segment of the movie. You can then cut, copy, and paste this segment using the Mac's keyboard, just as if it were text in a word processor. With this interface, it's easy to splice segments of many different movies together, and even to rearrange parts of a single movie. You can also make subtle changes, such as deleting one or two frames of a movie or doubling a frame here or there to achieve perfect synch with a sound track.

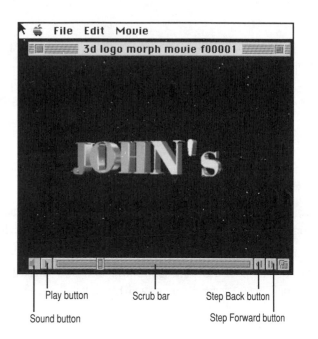

Figure 7.1
Movie Player

There are a number of useful options for Movie Player to change the way movies play back (see figure 7.2).

Figure 7.2
Movie Player options

Movie Player is much more than a means of playing your QuickTime movies, although it does that, too. Here are some things you can do with the Movie Player:

1. Open a movie and click on the Play button to play it. Click on the Pause button to pause it at the current frame during playback. The Step Forward button advances one frame at a time and the Step Back button steps backwards. Click on the left end of the Scrub bar to rewind to the start of the movie or on the right end of the Scrub bar to jump to the end.

Tip:
Hold the mouse on the Step Forward button to play a movie at the Mac's best rate without dropping any frames.

2. Drag the Scrub bar handle to riffle through the movie at variable speeds.

3. To cut, copy, or paste a frame, advance to that frame and pause the movie. Use the standard **Edit** menu or keyboard commands.

4. To select a range of frames to cut, copy, or paste, press Shift while you scrub over the frames with the Scrub bar.

5. When you cut a segment of QuickTime, adjacent segments are automatically spliced together. When you paste a segment, it is inserted immediately before the current frame.

6. Click on the Sound button to toggle sound on or off. Drag down on the speaker button to reduce or increase playback volume with the slider.

QuickFlix

Video Fusion Inc.
1722 Indian Wood Circle, Suite H
Maumee, OH 43537
Phone: (419) 891-1090 or (800) 638-5253
Fax: (419) 891-9673

Price: $149

System requirements: System 7.0.1 or later, 3M of RAM beyond system requirements (at least 4M recommended).

QuickFlix is Video Fusion's low-cost QuickTime editor, and it's a far cry from the basic Movie Player. You can use QuickFlix to edit together movies from many different sources, to add sound tracks to movies, and to smooth your edits with a wide variety of transitions. You can even add text titles to your movies and run effects filters over segments to create polarized or embossed segments.

You splice movies together by arranging them on a storyboard (see figure 7.3). These can then be rearranged by simply dragging icons to a new position on the storyboard.

128

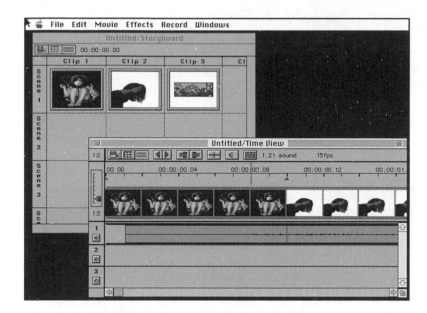

Figure 7.3
QuickFlix's storyboard

QuickFlix plays the segments by reading the storyboard left-to-right, top-to-bottom. Creating a dissolve or transition between two segments is as easy as selecting the two segments and choosing an effect (see figure 7.4). This is an intuitive use of a storyboard, and for traditional animators, it has a particularly familiar feel to it.

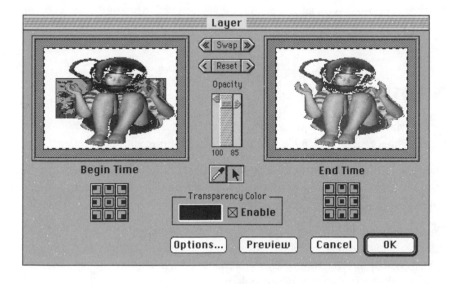

Figure 7.4
Creating a transition between two segments

129

The program has separate sound tracks, which let you mix several tracks of audio over your animation (including QuickTime movies that already contain sounds).

QuickFlix also offers many transitions, so you can smoothly join together multiple segments of animation.

While QuickFlix isn't an animation program, per se, it does let you create animated scrolling titles.

Movie Edit

MotionWorks USA
524 Second Street
San Francisco, CA 94107
Phone: (415) 541-9333 or (800) 800-8476
Fax: (415) 541-0555

Price: $249 (bundled with the Motion Works Utilities)

System requirements: not available

The Movie Edit is Movie Works's entry into the low-end QuickTime editor field. It can be used to edit together movies and add simple effects and sounds. Like the other programs in the Motion Works Utilities package, it wasn't ready for evaluation before *Cool Mac Animation* went to press.

Summary

People who spend their time creating QuickTime movies eventually (usually sooner than later) will want to edit their movies with sounds, transitions, and special effects.

The cheapest and easiest program for doing this is Apple's Movie Player, included free on the *Cool Animation Disk*. Other programs provide many more tools for working with sounds, filters, transitions, titles, and multiple layers.

Of course the combination of QuickTime, cool animation, and special effects and all the other bells and whistles described in previous chapters, will only wet the whistle of some animators. For this reason, the following chapter, "High-end Animation," scratches the surface of the bizarre and wonderful tools of the professional animator.

CHAPTER

High-end Animation

There are dozens of Mac tools used by professional animators that aren't described in detail in this book for the simple reason that they're expensive products and generally out of the reach of a beginning animator.

In the interest of letting you know what else is out there, however, we've included a short description of some of the best professional animation tools.

Professional animators are usually not satisfied with leaving their creations on the Mac. Their delivery platform of choice is generally film or video, and as such, professional animation tools are specially adapted to export finished animation on tape.

For video animators, Mac software offers a range of special features. These include *device control*, *field rendering*, *high-resolution output* and *time-code support*.

Device control is possibly the most complex of these special features. As the name implies, programs with this support control animation hardware, specifically, the video decks and special digital drives used for recording animations to video tape. Generally, this is only of concern to those with access to frame-accurate animation video decks or special digital tape drives such as the Exabyte 8500. These devices allow you to record animations one frame-at-a-time onto video tape.

Field rendering is term unique to video. Although video is commonly considered to play back at 30 frames per second, it's unfortunately not quite as simple as film. The catch is that video actually displays two fields for every frame of video. You can get an idea of how fields work by interlacing the fingers of both of your hands. The fingers of the left hand are known as the *even field* and the fingers of the right hand are the *odd field*. Video decks actually play back the even field, then the odd field in rapid succession before going to the next frame. When the even field is displayed, the odd field is black and vice versa. That's why if you look very closely at a TV screen, you'll see flickering horizontal black lines. The result is that you actually seeing two different pictures for every frame of video—in other words, 60 fps, not 30! Software that supports field rendering actually creates separate pictures for each subsequent field, resulting in animation that plays back twice as smoothly as animation that's recorded at a simple 30 fps.

High resolution output is a requirement for recording animations to film (recorders for 35mm film might have a resolution of 2,000-by-1,500 lines per inch—about 10 times as many pixels as video! Some have even higher resolution.)

Time code support is a requirement shared by video and film animators. Simply put, animation requires a special way of telling time. While we might be content to measure time in fractional seconds, an animator needs to specify time as a number of seconds and frames. For example, a film animator working at 24 fps expresses ten and one-third seconds as "10:08" or "ten seconds, eight frames." For a video animator (working at 30 fps) the same amount of time is expressed as 10:10 or ten seconds, ten frames. While this can be confusing at first, these are standard conventions supported by the film and television industries and they're known as SMPTE time code. If you're working with film, it's understood that a second is 24 frames; while video animators know that there are 30 frames in a second. If you have a sound track that's coded in SMPTE, it's crucial that you also have an animation program that works in this format so you don't have to constantly adjust your real-time animation to time-and-frames. (Keep in mind that animation for delivery from CD-ROM and other formats sometimes requires a frame rate of 15 fps or some other non-SMPTE standard which most animation software will be able to support as well).

Macromedia Director

Macromedia Inc.
600 Townsend Street
San Francisco, CA 94103
Phone: (800) 945-9355 or (415) 252-2000
Fax: (415) 626-0554

List price: $1,195

Director is one of the most popular animation programs on the Mac, but it's popularity has grown as much out of its animation tools as out of its tools for creating interactive multimedia presentations (see figure 8.1). Director allows you to create frame-based 2-D cel animations and export them as PICS, QuickTime, or stand-alone player applications.

Director's Cast window   Controller window   Main window or Stage

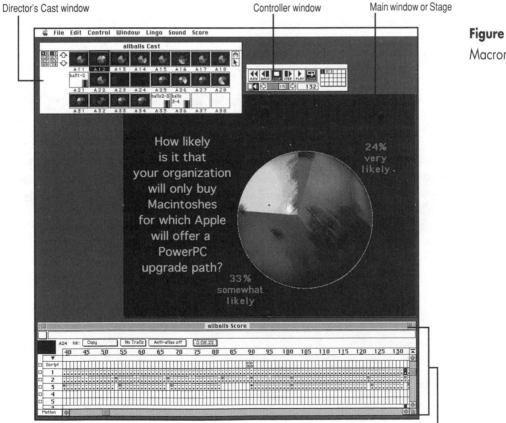

Figure 8.1
Macromedia Director

cel-based sequencer or Score

133

Like most computer animation systems, it allows for automatic tweening, layering, and mixing of animation and sound.

Like PROmotion, and other cel-animation systems, it features a simple painting module that enables you to step through cels as you create sprites. It also allows you to easily import artwork created in other programs.

With Director you can export animations as QuickTime movies, but it's best-suited to frame-by-frame presentations and it has better integrated support for PICS than it does for QuickTime.

Premiere

Adobe Systems Inc.
1585 Charleston Road
Mountain View, CA 94039-7900
Phone: (415) 961-4400

List price: $695 ($795 for deluxe CD-ROM edition)

Adobe's Premiere is probably the most powerful, therefore the most important, QuickTime application available. Think of it as a Swiss Army knife. No, better yet, think of it as a hardware store.

Premiere enables you to edit together movies and add animated titles, special effects, and transitions (see figure 8.2). Many animators will find Premiere indispensable when it comes time to splice together and tweak many little QuickTime tidbits, PICTs, and other odds and ends.

Premiere also has complete sound recording and mixing control, although it doesn't offer sound special effects (see figure 8.3).

It even lets you animate animations. If there's anything you want to do with existing QuickTime footage, chances are you can do it in Premiere.

The Titling tool is particularly cool because it enables you to animate the typographic qualities of a logo, such as height, width, weight, and size over time. Premiere automatically provides drop shadows, and you can adjust how dark and how far offset they are (see figure 8.4). Like any really good QuickTime program, Premiere is aware of alpha channels and uses them where appropriate.

One of its most important features is very good support for all kinds of different input and output hardware.

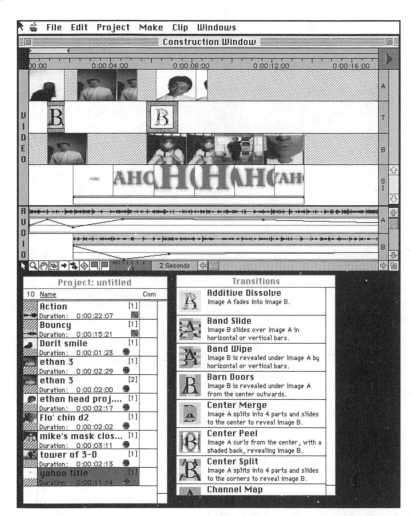

Figure 8.2

Premiere

135

Figure 8.3

Premiere's sound and mixing controls

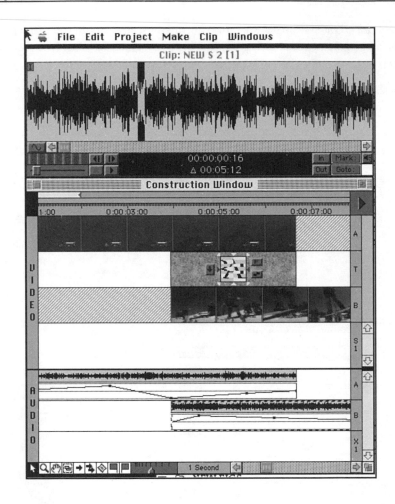

Figure 8.4

Using Premiere's Titling Tool

136

After Effects

CoSA *(a division of Aldus)*
14 Imperial Place, Suite 203
Providence, RI 02903
Phone: (401) 831-2672
Fax: (401) 831-2675

List price: $1,995

After Effects takes a much different approach to movie-making than Director. It specializes in creating broadcast-quality animations for video and relies on artwork created in other programs as a starting point.

After Effects isn't designed for creating character animation—you can't create sprites, for example—but it excels at making many layers of objects fly, spin, and dance across the screen (see figure 8.5). On the other hand, if you create your original artwork in a program that supports an alpha channel, such as Painter or Photoshop, you can create animations featuring your artwork as characters. After Effects excels at techniques like squashing, stretching, and enlarging layers with a minimum of image quality loss.

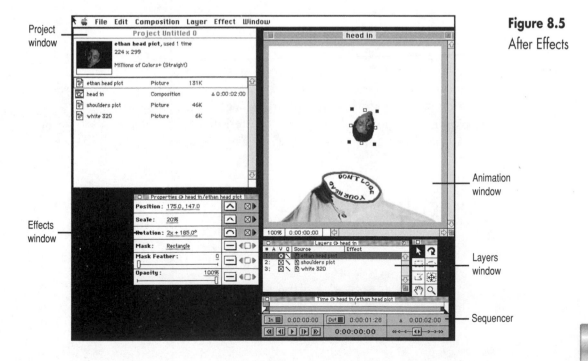

Figure 8.5
After Effects

137

Because After Effects is designed for output to video tape, it has many features demanded by video professionals, such as field rendering. It also has a capability called *sub-pixel rendering*, which means that motion is calculated much more precisely than the 72-dots-per-inch resolution of the Mac's display. This results in very smooth animations when outputting to high-quality video.

The program has sophisticated event-based animation that uses a 3-D style sequencer and includes effects like ease-in and ease out. It also offers optional hardware-assisted acceleration of effects.

Fortunately for the Cool Mac Animator, as this book was going to print, CoSA was planning to ship a multimedia version of After Effects. It will be missing many professional video production tools, but will cost less.

Animation Stand

Linker Systems
13612 Onkayha Circle
Irvine, CA 92720
Phone: (714) 552-1904
Fax (714) 552-6985

List price: $3,000

Linker Systems's professional animation tool has many features for professional video animators, such as device control and field rendering. It's a very complex program and few people will venture to learn to use it unless they're dedicated animation professionals. At $3,000, it's also one of the most expensive animation packages.

Macromedia 3D

Macromedia Inc.
600 Townsend Street
San Francisco, CA 94103
Phone: 800-945-9355 or 415-252-2000
Fax, 415-626-0554

List price: $1,495

Macromedia's 3-D animation system is a cross between the cel-based animation of Macromedia Director and the event-based, 3-D capabilities of Electric Image's Animation System. Macromedia 3D doesn't include a modeler, so in addition to a $1,495 animation package, you'll also need to invest in a capable modeler—running the price of 3-D animation up to about $3,000 or so.

Macromedia 3D uses a spreadsheet-style animation sequencer that gives you full control of animation parameters down to a very fine level of detail. For example, you can specify independent rotational values for the x, y, and z axes.

The program offers two kinds of rendering: Gouraud shading and direct support for Pixar's MacRenderMan. While Macromedia 3D is a cool program, we much prefer StrataStudio Pro from Strata Inc. because of its easier-to-use animation, simplified scene-building, and ray tracing.

Infini-D

Specular International Inc.
479 West Street
Amherst, MA 01002
Phone: (413) 253-3100
Fax: (413) 253-0540

List price: $895

As Specular International Inc.'s flagship 3-D animation software, Infini-D is very similar to LogoMotion, but adds a rich set of texture-mapping capabilities, more extensive modeling tools, a complete range of lighting types, and professional rendering capabilities, such as ray tracing.

In terms of navigation and interface, Infini-D looks and feels just like LogoMotion. This means you can start out with LogoMotion, and if your needs become more complex or demanding, you'll find it very easy to upgrade to Infini-D.

You can find the demo version of Infini-D on bulletin boards and online services, including the Hayden forum on CompuServe. See chapter 9, "Downloading Software."

Texture mapping is one of Infini-D's strongest features. You can combine many photographic images to create subtle or outrageous surfaces for objects.

Another important feature is ray tracing, which allows you to render very realistic reflections, shadows, and other natural effects.

Infini-D's modeling is mediocre for $800 software, but it's more powerful than LogoMotion's. You can build free-form objects by combining several profiles, and you can generate fractal terrains and other landscapes based on grayscale images.

StrataStudio Pro

Strata Inc.
2 West St. George Boulevard, Suite 2100
St. George, UT 84770
Phone: (800) 678-7282
Fax: (801) 628-9756

List price: $1,495

StrataStudio Pro is by far the coolest of the integrated 3-D modelers and animators available to Mac users. It features a complete 3-D modeler that includes spline modeling and unusual shapes such as sweeps (snail shells and other spirals), terrains generated from grayscale images, and free-form polygonal shapes (see figure 8.6).

Figure 8.6

Modeling with
StrataStudio Pro

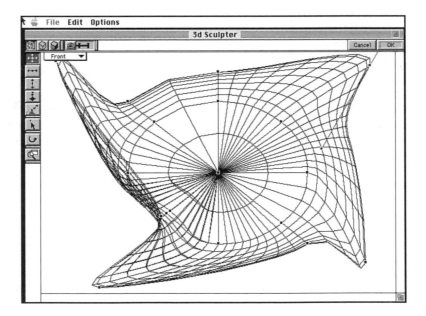

The scene building tools include a rich lighting palette, fantastic texture mapping tools, and easy navigation in three dimensions (see figure 8.7).

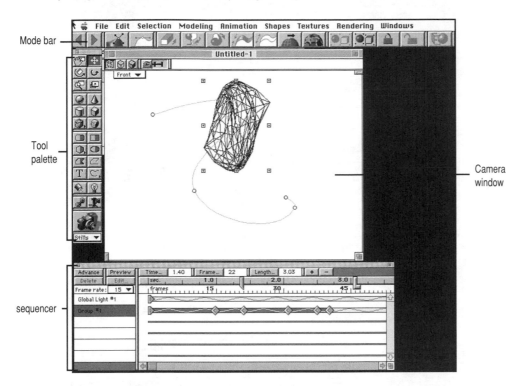

Mode bar

Tool palette

sequencer

Camera window

StrataStudio Pro's texture-mapping features enable you to apply photographic images directly to the surface of objects (you could map a picture of fish scales onto the model of a airplane, for example). It has tools for doing this very precisely (see figures 8.8 and 8.9), so you can even map windows onto the sides of a rocket or text labels onto a control panel.

Animation is where StrataStudio really shines. Like Infini-D, it uses an event-based sequencer. There are many extra features, however. As you move an object from event to event, a spline animation path is generated that connects the dots representing each event. You can drag these event marks around in 3-D space and directly modify the splines that make up the animation path. You are not limited to modifying the path in one view. For instance, you can modify the motion curve in the front view, switch to the top view and tweak it around even further. The result is that objects are easily animated along any path in 3-D space.

Something else StrataStudio Pro has going for it is excellent ray-traced rendering, in addition to the standard Phong, Gouraud, and other fast rendering methods commonly employed by

Figure 8.8

StrataStudio Pro's texture mapping window allows you to precisely position and scale textures.

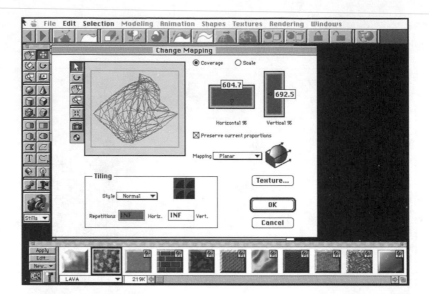

Figure 8.9

StrataStudio Pro's Expert Texture Editing window

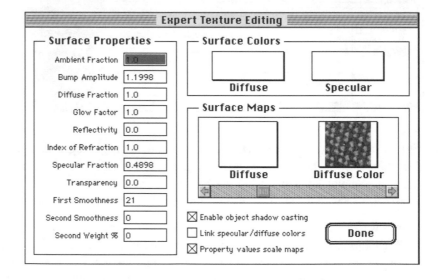

animators. Although ray tracing is comparatively slow, it's great when you need mirror reflections, refraction through glass, and other photorealistic effects.

One of the really cool, if gimmicky, features of StrataStudio Pro is particle animation, meaning you can explode a model into bits and have the particles reform into a new shape (see figure 8.10).

Another really cool capability is making an animated object follow a path. With standard path

Figure 8.10
StrataStudio Pro's explode!
dialog.

animation and tweening techniques, when you make a car race around an oval track, it first goes forward, then sideways, then backwards, then sideways again in relation to its direction of travel. This isn't very realistic. StrataStudio Pro lets you set the car to turn as it rounds the corners. You can also set it to bank as it goes through turns, just like an airplane (see figure 8.11).

Figure 8.11
Banking through
turns in StrataStudio
Pro

Electric Image Animation System

Electric Image Inc.
117 East Colorado Boulevard, Suite 300
Pasadena, CA 91105
Phone: (818) 577-1627
Fax: (818) 577-2426

List price: $7,495

Electric Image's Animation System (most pros call it Electric Image) is the crowned prince of Mac animation. Not only is it the most powerful animation tool available on the Mac, but it's also the most expensive ($7,495) making it a tool for serious, hard-core professionals only.

EIAS does one thing extremely well: 3-D animation. It's not a modeler, although it generates excellent 3-D models from type.

Once you've imported your 3-D models into EIAS (Autodessys Inc.'s Form•Z is a very popular choice of modelers), you set them in motion by moving the time marker in the sequencer and moving or changing models to create new events (see figure 8.12).

Figure 8.12

Electric Image Animation System's sequencer

tools

Outline view of model parts being animated

Specify the values for each part over time

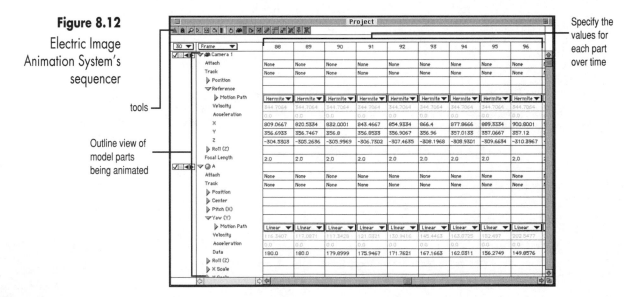

EIAS uses an animation metaphor that's derived from traditional movie-camera operations. As such, it's very easy to animate the camera which defines your point of view.

This is the only program to date that allows you to define changes in animation parameters by adjusting spline curves. While other 3-D sequencers limit you to time or numeric displays of parameters such as position and rotation, EIAS can display a timeline where every parameter down to acceleration over individual axes is displayed in the form of a curve. In places where you increase the slope of the curve, the value increases more rapidly, where the curve is flat, the value remains static, and so on.

One of EIAS's strongest features is device control. If you happen to be animating directly to a professional animation video deck, EIAS will control it directly, automatically advancing the tape one frame for each new frame of animation. EIAS also supports field rendering, and it has many presets for animating to film, and video, among other professional formats.

DeBabelizer

Equilibrium Inc.
475 Gate Five Road, Suite 225
Sausalito, CA 94965
Phone: (415) 332-4343
Fax: (415) 332-4433

List price: $299 (formats packages for some special file formats are extra).

DeBabelizer is not really an animation program at all, but if you're a hard-core animator, you'll want to own a copy anyway. DeBabelizer is a *batch image processor*. What does this mean? It means you can have a folder full of images — hundreds or thousands of them, even — and the program can perform a series of actions on every one of them with only a single command from you. For example, you might have a folder full of scanned-in hand drawings saved as PICTs and simply numbered 1 through 1,000. You can have DeBabelizer open every one of the images and append it, in sequence, to the end of a QuickTime movie called "Finished Movie." Since DeBabelizer will open and save almost any image format, including animation formats, you could have it convert a hard disk full of PICS files to QuickTime movies or vice versa (see figure 8.13).

Since many computer animators have to concern themselves with the creation of animations

Figure 8.13

Performing a batch
save with
DeBabelizer

File   Edit   Palette   Misc   Scripts

DeBabelizer   **control panel spare**

control panel spare

                    Original Current
Wide : 320   320
Hi :   240   240
Color : 17Mil 17Mil
DPI : 72   72

RGB:
HSV:
XYI:

[Cancel]
[Options...]
[Next Image]

Batch Save

[New...] [Edit...] [Delete]

List: Sean's batch list   ▼

□ Bananas
□ Clouds.mov
□ control panel spare

● Open   ALL   ▼
○ Acquire   Anti-aliased PICT... ▼
            Automatic   ▼

□ Don't go into subfolders

For each image in List:
• Do Script: NOTHING   ▼
• Display: Stop and wait   ▼
• Save: [Auto Naming Options...]
  ● To: [Set...] UltraDrive 1000S :
  ○ To: Folder image came from
  ○ To: Manually select
  Type: PICT2   ▼ PICS (animation)
  Colors: 17M (24 bits)   ▼ ⊠ Auto set
  □ Slice...   ⊠ Verify replace
  □ Picture Preview   □ 1 image/file
  □ Picture Icon   ⊠ 1 animation/file
  ⊠ Bypass warning messages
  □ Hit OK in unattended dialogs

[OK] [Cancel] [Exit with settings] [Help...]

that will be played back on computers with specific color palettes, DeBabelizer can reduce
a full-color animation to an 8-bit or some other color palette. Each image in the animation
will have only pixels drawn from the same "super palette" (see figure 8.14).

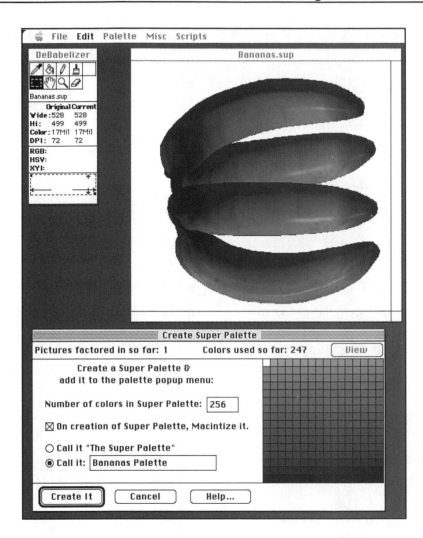

Figure 8.14
Creating a super palette

The variety of uses for DeBabelizer is unlimited. No sane professional Mac animator will try to go through life without it. On the other hand, it's not a very friendly program because hundreds of features are crammed together. But those who unlock its features become digital masters. Since it's impossible to *fully* define what DeBabelizer does, here is a list of ten things it can do:

1. Open every image in a folder or volume and save it in another location in a different file format.

2. Reduce or crop a batch of images to a specific size.

3. Reduce the palette of every 24-bit image in a folder to 8-bits, optimized so that each image has a "vote" on which colors will produce the best results.

4. Reduce the color palette of every frame to share a single palette used by one image.

5. Convert a folder full of PICS files to a folder full of QuickTime movies.

6. Remove all of the green (any shade) pixels from the background of every frame of an animation.

7. Composite a folder full of images with alpha channels over another folder full of background images.

8. Apply a Photoshop Emboss filter to every frame of a digitized video.

9. Convert every frame of a movie to numbered PICT files for rotoscoping in a paint program, then convert them all back into a QuickTime movie

10. Using AppleScript and a video frame grabber, create a program that causes DeBabelizer to acquire an image every 30 minutes from a video camera and append it to a time-lapse digital QuickTime movie.

Working Model

Knowledge Revolution
15 Brush Place
San Francisco, CA 94103
Phone: (415) 553-8153
Fax: (415) 553-8012

List price: $995

Working Model was not designed with the animator in mind. Instead, this program is dedicated to creating accurate physics simulations using complex mathematical formulae. For the Mac animator, that point is secondary. Working Model is a tremendous boon to anyone who needs to create animations the follow the laws of physics. For example, you can easily create an animation that resembles a complex Rube Goldberg or Wyle E. Coyote machine. Balls can roll down ramps and knock over pins which can release levers which ignite explosions that move huge weights to tumble over cliffs…and so on (see figure 8.15). Of course, you can also create animations of helium-filled logos floating up and blowing away in the wind.

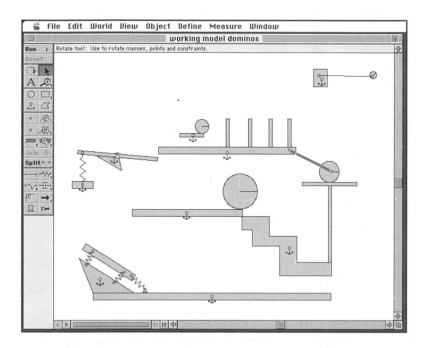

Figure 8.15
A Rube Goldberg machine in Working Model

Two things define Working Model's unique animation capabilities: *inverse kinematics* and *physical modeling*. Inverse kinematics means that objects are automatically interrelated. For example, if you create an arm connected to a forearm connected to a hand connected to a finger—all using rotational joints—pulling on the finger will cause the arm to straighten and follow naturally; on the other hand (get it?) if you raise the arm at the shoulder, the forearm, hand, and finger will raise without changing their orientation.

Physical modeling means that every object follows the laws of physics (those you choose to apply). For example, if you place several objects on the screen without anchoring them in place, and click the "Go" button, they will all accelerate and fall according to the normal laws of gravity. (Of course, you can set gravity to that of the moon, Jupiter, or outer space, if you desire.) If you anchor a floor at the bottom of the screen and drop a rubber ball on it from the top of the screen, it will automatically bounce up, fall down, and bounce up realistically until it comes to a stop naturally.

Exabyte/Abekas Drivers

Abekas
ASDG Software Inc.
925 Stewart Street
Madison, WI 53713
Phone: (608) 273-6585
Fax: (608) 271-1988

List price: $495

System requirements: System 7.01 or later 8M RAM, Exabyte 8500 or 8505

The Missing Link
Knoll Software Inc.
P.O. Box 6887
San Rafael, CA 94903-0887
Phone: (415) 453-2471
Fax: (415) 453-2471

There are two competing programs that do such similar things, that it seems appropriate to cover them simultaneously.

The Abekas driver from ASDG Inc. and The Missing Link, from Knoll Software, are both designed to allow you to use an Exabyte tape drive as a transport mechanism for taking your animations to a service bureau for output to video tape. The link provided by the service bureau is the super-high-end Abekas video system. This is the top-of-the-line digital video recording system. Basically, it enables you to record your Mac generated animations to professional-quality analog video tape with no loss of quality.

Exabyte drives are practically free when compared to the $100,000-or-so Abekas systems. You can pick up an Exabyte deck for around $1,000 and the tapes are only about $10 each. Once you've transferred your animation to the Exabyte tape, you simply bring it down to the local video service bureau, and for a reasonable fee, have the animation output a frame at a time to professional tape, such as D-1 or Beta SP. The service bureau will usually handle dubbing to VHS or whatever other format you're using, as well. This is an outstanding, and affordable, way for low-budget animators to get started generating big-budget productions.

Summary

High-end animation software enables you to do many things you can do in the low-end programs, but it also provides very fine control over animation parameters, and sometimes provides for things like hardware control for people putting animations on film or video. Learning the high-end programs is a commitment, as is the cost of the required hardware and software. However, the results you can get from these programs rival anything you'll see on television.

For those interested in exploring some of these programs, demo versions are available from Hayden's online forum on CompuServe. See the next chapter, "Downloading Software" for an explanation of how to get copies of these programs, as well as sample files used in this book.

Downloading Software

This chapter attempts to get you started on downloading software to further your Mac animation career. Included in the Hayden Books forum on CompuServe are demo versions of cool Mac animation software, an FPU simulation utility, and example files from the *Cool Mac Animation* chapters. The following is a list of things to look for (in case the *Cool Animation Disk* just isn't enough).

PROmotion Demo

PROMOT.SEA

This demo version of Motion Works's PROmotion has been around for a while, but it's still a cool introduction to cel animation. You can create and play back animations in a single session, or open and play back existing animations, but you can't save your work for future use. The archive includes some sample animations.

Infini-D Demo

INFIND.SEA

The demo version of Specular's Infini-D is unique in that it allows you to actually create rendered still images and QuickTime animations. The catch is that they're limited to 320-by-240 pixels, but it's still a great way to delve into 3-D modeling and animation. Like other demo software, it lets you open existing model and animation files. This archive includes sample animations and 3-D models.

Working Model Demo

WORKMO.SEA

This program is the only thing available on the Mac that gives you true, physics-based animation and inverse kinematics. It's a pretty sophisticated program, suitable for engineers and lawyers, but animators will love being able to create animations driven by gravity, elasticity, friction, wind, and other forces of nature. The demo version lets you explore the program without saving your work. It includes sample animations in QuickTime format and working models.

Cinemation Demo

CINEMA.SEA

The demo version of Cinemation allows you to create cel-based animations and interactive presentations, but not to save your work. The archive includes sample animations.

StrataStudio Pro Demo

SSPRO.SEA

StrataStudio Pro is one of the coolest high-end 3-D modeling/rendering/animation programs available on the Mac. The demo version lets you do everything but save your work. It includes sample animations in QuickTime format and sample 3-D models.

Cool Mac Animation Examples

CMA01, CMA02, etc.

The forum includes cool sample animations from the *Cool Mac Animation* chapters and the files used to create them. The archives are labeled CMA01, CMA02, and so on, according to the chapters the samples came from.

Flip Book

Of course the Hayden Book forum includes the flip book animation from *Cool Mac Animation*, all in full-color QuickTime format.

Re-animator

REANIM.SEA

This very simple freeware program enables you to play back PICS files without any other applications. Think of it as a MoviePlayer for those without QuickTime.

FPU

FPU.SEA

Don't miss out on this shareware floating-point coprocessor simulator for use in non-FPU Macs. If you use this program, you'll need to pay the $15 shareware fee to its creator.

How to Download

If you've ever downloaded files from CompuServe, you'll find it easy to access these archives. When you log on to CompuServe, type Go Hayden at the prompt; this takes you directly to Hayden's forum. Here you will find the archives shown above in italics.

The procedure for downloading depends on your connection software. Refer to your software and CompuServe manuals for explicit instructions.

Once you have downloaded a file to your hard disk, double-click on the archive and specify a location and name for the files on your disk. When an archive contains multiple files, they're all in a single folder.

CHAPTER

Cool
Mac

Glossary

A

Actor   Also called a character or sprite, an actor is a single figure made up of multiple cels to simulate natural motion.

Alpha channel   A mask present in some 32-bit images and animations; it allows you to seamlessly combine foreground and background images.

Animation deck   An expensive VCR-style video deck that enables you to record one frame of animation at a time.

Artifacts   In image processing, this refers to small defects in quality due to digital processing and compression.

B

Batch processor   DeBabelizer is the best example: it performs one or more actions on a whole group of images or animations. Some QuickTime programs also feature batch import.

Bevels   The detailing on the edges of 3-D objects. These provide highlights, and realism.

Byte   A byte is 8 bits of information; a kilobyte (K) is 1,000 bytes, and a megabyte (M) is 1,000 kilobytes.

C

Character   *See* **Actor**.

Clock speed   Refers to the clock that controls the timing of your Mac's CPU. For a given CPU, speed is proportional to the clock speed.

Compression   The technique used to squeeze images and sounds into much less disk space than normally required. QuickTime compression makes it possible to play animations at video frame rates from your Mac.

Compressors   A number of different compressors are available for QuickTime, depending on the application and hardware you're using. For example, the Animation compressor saves only the changes between subsequent frames.

Cycling   Also called looping, this technique plays a segment of animation or a multi-cel character over and over to create a long animation.

D

Device control   The control of professional video hardware by your Mac.

Digital signal processor   Usually called DSP, this is a chip (usually on a NuBus board) that speeds the analog-to-digital conversion of signals. It's also used to accelerate some all-digital processes.

Digitize   To convert analog information, such as video, pictures, or sounds, into a digital format. This usually requires special hardware, such as frame grabbers, scanners, or sound samplers.

Displacement Effect used by Pixar's shaders to create bumps on an object's surface.

Drop frames Technique used by QuickTime to adhere to the timing of a movie. If QuickTime can't play all of the frames, it drops occasional frames to avoid slowing down.

E

Event-based animation Relies on changes to individual objects or characters and tweens the changes to characters independently of other characters.

Extrusion The cookie-cutter technique of forming 3-D shapes from an outline.

F

Field rendering Creating separate frames of an animation for the even and odd fields of a single frame of video.

Focal length 3-D software's simulation of a real-world camera lens. A long lens is telephoto and has a narrow angle of view. A short lens is wide angle, meaning it sees a very wide field, but results in some distortion.

Frame rate The speed at which frames of an animation are played. Usually described as frames per second (fps), typical rates are 15 fps for Mac delivery of compact video, 24 fps for motion picture film, and 30 fps for NTSC video.

Frames This is a single image in an animation made up of many sequential images.

G

Gel A colored plastic filter placed over a light.

Gouraud A smooth-shading rendering technique used by LogoMotion that results in realistically shaded surfaces, but does not support detailed textures.

H

Hierarchical motion Sometimes called parent-child animation, this allows a child object's motion to be tied to the parent object's motion. It's a hierarchy because a child can also be a parent to another object.

I

Inverse kinematics   A technique supported by Working Model and other high-end programs, in which the motion of a child object in a hierarchical structure is reflected in the parent according structural rules, e.g., pull on the finger and the shoulder moves slightly.

K

Key-frame animation   A key frame defines the overall state of an the animation at a point in time. When multiple key frames are defined, animation software will calculate a smooth animation from one key frame to the next.

Kinetograph   Thomas Edison's first motion picture camera.

Kinetoscope   Edison's companion product, the first projector.

L

Lathing   The creation of a 3-D object by revolving an outline around an axis.

Layering   The superimposition of one character over another.

Looping   *See* **Cycling**.

M

Mask   *See* **Alpha channel**.

Megabyte   *See* **Byte**.

Model sheet   A piece of paper that shows a character in many postures and expressions. Used to consistently define a character for multiple animators working separately.

Morphing   The seemingly magical blending of one image into another.

N

Numbered PICT   A file format consisting of PICT files numbered in order.

160

O

Onion skinning A technique offered by some animation programs that allows you to see an earlier cel of a character while you work on the current one.

P

Path animation Allows you to animate a character by drawing its motion path on the screen.

Physical modeling and animation The creation and animation of shapes according to the laws of physics. This results in very natural motion.

Procedural shaders Texture format used by Pixar and other 3-D companies for creating surface textures according to algorithms, rather than photos.

Publisher and subscribe System 7's technology for automatically sharing and updating a single file between two or more programs.

R

RAM Random access memory. The chips in your Mac that enable it to store information. A typical Mac has 4M of RAM, but animators usually require 8M or more.

Ray tracing A photorealistic rendering technique that accurately depicts reflections, refraction, shadows, and other effects of light. Available only in high-end 3-D animation programs.

Reflection environment An image that simulates a real-world environment when rendering in 3-D. Required to realistically depict metals and other reflective surfaces.

Registration point The spot at which a cel of animation aligns with previous and subsequent cels.

Rotoscoping This refers, in general, to painting on frames of video. Motion Works's Motion Paint is specifically designed for this, but other programs allow it with work-arounds.

S

Script   The document that describes an animation, including dialogue, action, and background information.

Sprite   *See* **Actor**.

Storyboard   A thumbnail view of an animation used to plan important events and action. Resembles a comic strip.

Stroboscope   A spinning wheel with slots and painted animation cels used to view simple animations in a mirror.

Sub-pixel rendering   The rendering of motion smaller than the Mac's screen resolution of 72 dots per inch. Used when super-smooth animation is required.

T

Time code   The standard measure of time used by video and film professionals, usually expressed as hours:minutes:seconds:frames. It is understood that film uses 24 frames per second and video uses 30 frames per second.

Tweening   Also called in-betweening, it is the automatic calculation of frames in between two key frames or events.

Type string   A trumped-up computerese expression meaning "word."

W

Warping   The stretching, twisting, and taffy-like manipulation of images.

Z

Zeotrope   A device contemporary with the stroboscope that allowed pre-movie people to view animations.

Index

M